Relational Aggression in Girls

A Prevention and Intervention Curriculum with Activities & Lessons for Small Groups and Classsrooms

By Jamie Kupkovits, Ed.S., NCSP

(Grades 4 – 12)

© 2008 by YouthLight, Inc.
Chapin, SC 29036

Cover Design and Layout by Rebecca Gray
Edited by Susan Bowman

ISBN: 1-59850-055-4
EAN:978-1-59850-055-4

Library of Congress Control Number: 2008926979

10 9 8 7 6 5 4 3 2 1
Printed in the United States

youth light inc.

PO Box 115 • Chapin, SC 29036
(800) 209-9774 • (803)345-1070 • Fax (803)345-0888
yl@youthlightbooks.com • www.youthlightbooks.com

Dedication

To my family with the utmost love and gratitude –

For my husband, Thor, who keeps me laughing and balanced

For my parents, Julie and Brad, who have supported me in all of my endeavors

To my little buddy, Lauren –

Your young life is a constant reminder to live every day with passion and purpose

"For from Him and through Him and to Him are all things..."

— Romans 11:36

Acknowledgements

I continue to be amazed at how blessed I am. I could not have written nor completed this project without the loving support and encouragement from my family and friends. I would like to thank my husband who has continuously given me the encouragement to reach higher, the inspiration to pursue my dreams, and the strength to keep me balanced. I would also like to thank my parents for their words of wisdom and the sacrifices they have made in order to give me the opportunities to achieve my goals and aspirations. Thank you to my brother and sister who continually remind me to laugh and enjoy every day for what it brings.

Thank you to those individuals who have come into my life and have inspired me to help others through their willingness to help me. I would especially like to thank those teachers who were willing to see, listen, and offer their compassion. Thank you, Mrs. Gerndt.

Thank you to colleagues who have always been willing to share their knowledge and generosity. I would especially like to thank Dr. Jim Larson and the school psychology department at the University of Wisconsin-Whitewater for their tireless commitment to their lifelong graduate students. Thank you for your willingness to continuously offer your knowledge, advice, and guidance. Thank you to colleagues who have encouraged me to take my knowledge of relational aggression to a higher level and who have provided me with feedback about the program.

Thank you to the students I have worked with and have allowed me to be a part of their lives. Their stories of struggle, triumph, and resiliency are the true stories of heroism that we all can learn from. Your stories inspire us to make a difference.

Table of Contents

Relational Aggression Curriculum Summary Statement

This curriculum has been designed based on what the available research has found works for girls who are relationally aggressive. This curriculum contains objectives and goals that have been suggested to be effective based on this research. Specific objectives and activities are included for each of the nine week sessions. An additional, or follow-up, session is also included to further assess whether any long term effects from the curriculum are evident. To date, this curriculum has been used as a prevention tool using a classroom-wide format. However, a screening form to help identify students in need of treatment for small group intervention is also included. An assessment measure is strongly encouraged to be used as a pretest and posttest measure to evaluate change in perceptions, beliefs, and knowledge regarding relational aggression. This curriculum has been designed as a school-based intervention program and can be implemented by trained professionals including school psychologists, social workers, counselors, as well as teachers. Other trained mental health providers may find some of the techniques and strategies helpful as well.

General Objectives and Goals:

- Define and provide examples of relational aggression
- Learn and use strategies for dealing with relational aggression
  - Challenging Negative Belief Systems about Girl Behaviors:
    - Defining Normative Beliefs about Relational Aggression
    - Identifying Thoughts, Feelings, and Actions Associated with Relational Aggression
    - Problem Solving Situations that Involve Relational Aggression
    - Role Playing
  - Assertiveness Skills and Strategies:
    - Assertiveness Awareness
    - Role Playing with Assertiveness Skills
    - Behavior Contracts or Promises
    - Healthy Friendship Skills and Strategies
  - Self-Esteem and Self-Confidence Building:
    - Emotional Development
    - Empathy Training
    - Perspective Taking and Understanding Differences
    - Self-Esteem and Self-Talk
    - Goal Setting
    - Mentoring

How to Use this Curriculum

This curriculum was designed with the intent to help school children understand and deal with relational aggression. Limited school resources currently exist that are based on research regarding relational aggression. The present curriculum has attempted to include many of the objectives according to the available research for addressing and treating relational aggression.

This curriculum was specifically developed for school psychologists, counselors, and social workers to use with children in a school-based setting. However, outside mental health providers may find the strategies within the curriculum helpful in treating the youth they see who are struggling with issues related to relational aggression and bullying. This intervention has been developed, researched, and evaluated for practical use within the school system. Field testing of this program has indicated an increase in knowledge, including strategy use, of relational aggression following the posttest assessment and completion of the nine week intervention program.

A single subject design was conducted using 11 sixth grade girls from a Midwestern region in Southeastern Wisconsin. These girls were given the *Relational Aggression Assessment Measure (Knowledge Test and Beliefs Test)* prior to implementation of the nine sessions and again following the ninth group session. Although incidences of relational aggression were present among this group according to teacher reports, intensive intervention was not warranted. Therefore, this program was implemented at the prevention level for increasing awareness and knowledge about relational aggression. Non-parametric methods (i.e. graphic analysis or inspection) were used in order to analyze results. It was hypothesized that an increase on the *Relational Aggression Assessment Measure – Knowledge Test* would indicate an increased awareness and knowledge of relational aggression, and an increase on the *Beliefs Test* would indicate more prosocial beliefs about relational aggression. About 73% of the girls who received this curriculum obtained results consistent with the proposed hypothesis on the *Knowledge Test,* suggesting that a majority of the girls showed an increase in their knowledge and strategy use of relational aggression. Upon closer inspection, 62% indicated a substantial score increase from pretest to posttest. About 64% of the girls showed an increase or had the same score from pretest to posttest on the *Beliefs Test,* possibly indicating that some girls demonstrated an increase in their prosocial beliefs while others already demonstrated more favorable beliefs about relational aggression prior to implementation of the curriculum.

The above study was replicated again the following school year this time with 25 girls from two sixth grade classrooms from a Midwestern region in Southeastern Wisconsin. It was again expected that girls would demonstrate an increase on the *Relational Aggression Assessment Measure – Knowledge and Beliefs Tests.* All girls who completed this curriculum showed some increase from their pretest to posttest scores on either the *Knowledge or Beliefs Test.* About 92% of the girls showed an increase in their knowledge and strategy use of relational aggression, while about 60% showed an increase in more prosocial beliefs about relational aggression.

Relational aggression is often seen as the dominant form of bullying for girls and experts agree that boys are also likely to use forms of relational aggression in addition to physical forms of bullying (Crick and Grotpeter, 1995). To date, this curriculum has been implemented within a classroom setting consisting of female students. It is probable, however, that boys may also benefit from being taught some of the strategies in this intervention manual. A classroom-wide format has been chosen as the preferred method of implementation for this program due to the nature of relational aggression, as the aggressors of relational aggression can often later become victims. Using a classroom-wide format may help to eliminate a bully vs. victim dynamic that could be present in a small group format.

This curriculum has been designed for students in the upper elementary grades to the high school level (i.e. grades 4-12). The author has used and has found the following format to be one way to implement this intervention in an elementary school setting. Designate two individuals to serve as group leaders. Leaders can be student services staff and/or teaching staff. It is always preferable to have the students' teachers involved in the group sessions in order to better promote generalization of strategies learned throughout the group. This way, teachers can remind and reteach the concepts learned throughout the school day. Divide the boys and girls into two classroom groups, and designate a facilitator for each group. Use the present curriculum for the girls' classroom group in order to focus specifically on relational aggression awareness and intervention strategies. Use another bullying curriculum for the boys' classroom group. Possible curriculums might include *Bully Proofing Your School: A Comprehensive Approach for Elementary Schools* (Sopris West, 1994) or *Bully Proofing Your School: A Comprehensive Approach for Middle Schools* (Sopris West, 2000). Both of these resources have been demonstrated to be effective in decreasing bullying according to the research literature. Following implementation of the nine week sessions, a tenth week can be added. During this time, have the boys and girls present and share their knowledge of bullying to one another. It is suggested that the girls and boys develop projects about the different forms of bullying that can be presented to their classmates during this tenth week (see session one – group projects).

Each of the nine sessions intends to teach girls the vocabulary and strategies of relational aggression. A follow up session is included in order to measure any long term effects or changes following implementation of the curriculum. Each of the nine sessions teaches girls about relational aggression using direct instruction techniques and active learning activities. A relational aggression book study has been incorporated into each of the sessions in order to help girls understand and empathize with others affected by relational aggression. Homework activities are also included at the end of each session in order to help the girls transfer and generalize the information learned from the group sessions. It may be helpful for each girl to be given a folder where the homework pages, as well as any reproducible pages, can be kept.

Included in Appendix B is the *Relational Aggression Assessment Measure – Knowledge and Beliefs Test*. It is strongly encouraged that this assessment be used in order to understand how much girls know about relational aggression prior to implementation of the curriculum. Also, giving this assessment measure will help to understand what the girls' current beliefs are regarding relationally aggressive behaviors. Give this assessment during the first group session and again following implementation of the curriculum during the last group session to determine if the girls demonstrated a change in their knowledge and beliefs about relational aggression. For group leaders desiring to use this program as a small group intervention, a small group screening form can be used. This screening form is located in Appendix D.

Background Research

Aggression in school-aged children has often been a topic of interest in both past and recent research literature. According to Larson and Lochman (2002), children with aggression problems are likely to be evident in five to ten percent of children. Most concerning is the detrimental effects that can manifest when aggression problems in children are left untreated. Engagement in aggressive behaviors early in childhood has been established by researchers to be a significant risk factor for the presence of aggression in later adulthood (Hinshaw & Lee, 2003). Children with aggression problems may be more likely to be referred for special education services and are more likely to be retained and eventually suspended, all of which are likely to lead to underachievement in school (Hinshaw & Lee, 2003).

Once viewed as solely characteristic of the male population, researchers are currently examining the differences in aggression between boys and girls (i.e. Phelps, 2001; Crick & Grotpeter, 1995). Aggression, often defined as being physical and overt, has taken on a new definition when exploring female social hierarchies. Simmons (2002) found that aggressive behaviors exhibited by girls are likely to manifest to a different degree when compared to the aggression demonstrated by their male counterparts. Researchers have suggested that girls have learned that the expression of anger is socially undesirable to display, and engagement in physical acts of aggression is socially discouraged (Pipher, 1994). Taught to reject open or direct conflict, girls revert to using indirect and nonphysical aggression with one another (Simmons, 2002).

Past researchers have often looked toward physical, direct acts to define aggression while ignoring more indirect, unobservable forms of aggression (Simmons, 2002). Such aggression may often go undetected and ignored due to its covert and sophisticated nature (Yoon, Barton, & Tairiol, 2004). This form of aggression has also gone undetected because it defies the conventional terms that are often used to describe bullying (Simmons, 2002). Schools have often been observed as not including such behaviors in anti-bullying policies that reject bullying, because this type of aggression is often seen as being unconventional from physical and overt bullying (Simmons, 2002). Therefore, it is increasingly important for other forms of aversive peer behaviors, aside from physical acts, to be identified in children and adolescents in order to avoid missing subgroup behaviors of aggression in youth (Cullerton-Sen & Crick, 2005).

Researchers have recently come to define such covert forms of aggression as relational aggression. Crick and Grotpeter (1995) have defined relational aggression as a distinct form of aggression that includes damaging or hurting others by manipulating social relationships in a purposeful manner. It is friendship that becomes the weapon, while body language and relationship associations become the fighting mechanisms (Simmons, 2002). Relational aggression is further defined as an imbalance of power that intends to damage peer group relationships and reputations in order to strengthen one's power and social status (Mullin-Rindler, 2003). It is the control over another individual in a relationship that one is actively engaged in being relationally aggressive (Simmons, 2002).

Relational aggression is often described as being indirect, or covertly inflicting harm upon another, such as excluding or spreading rumors about others (Simmons, 2002; Nixon, 2005). Such indirect or covert behaviors also seek to harm the self-esteem and peer status of others (Simmons, 2002). Researchers have further defined relational aggression as female bullying (Dellasega & Nixon, 2003; Simmons, 2002) that has become disparaging and widespread (Simmons, 2002). However, the term bullying is often disregarded by observers and those who engage in relational aggression, because it is considered to be part of the anguish that goes along with friendships (Simmons, 2002).

In addition to spreading rumors and excluding others, relational aggression also consists of backstabbing, ignoring or giving others the silent treatment, creating clubs designed to isolate others, insulting others through verbal means, and acts of body language that are hostile in nature (Nixon, 2005; Simmons, 2002; Skowronski et al., 2005). It is often through nonverbal body language or gestures, or the act of giving one mean looks, excluding others, and giving the silent treatment, in which relational aggression often flourishes (Simmons, 2002).

The definition of relational aggression has also expanded to include a term called cyber bullying. It is through the use of the computer in which children spread rumors about each other, send harassing or embarrassing emails to a mass number of people, and steal the on line identities of one another (Dellasega & Nixon, 2003; Skowronski et al., 2005; The Ophelia Project, 2005). Phone conversations, specifically three way calls, can also increase the chance for indirect aggression to take place, as one girl may be encouraged to talk about another girl when the girl is in fact listening to the conversation (Dellasega & Nixon, 2003).

Such techniques have been seen as advantageous to use by individuals because aggressors are void of directly confronting their victims (Skowronski et al., 2005). Using the silent treatment, for example, is one method that aggressors can quickly and indirectly use to attack others (Simmons, 2002). Dellasega and Nixon (2003) stated that such opportunities for the exhibition of indirect or anonymous aggressive acts reduces the likelihood that aggressors will be accountable and responsible for their actions. On the other hand, the targets of relational aggression begin to feel a sense of blame for the undesirable situation, as they are unable to work out the conflict directly and are not allowed the chance to express their concerns to others (Simmons, 2002).

According to available research regarding ethnic diversity, relational aggression appears to affect all ethnicities (Prinstein, Boergers, & Vernberg, 2001) and is not only characteristic of individuals in the United States (Dellasega & Nixon, 2003). However, data is currently lacking regarding observable differences among people from various locations or economics (Dellasega & Nixon, 2003). As with many risk factors and detrimental effects, research does indicate that relational aggression may be affected by socioeconomic status. For example, girls with lower socioeconomic status, for example, may present with a lower sense of security and may further define themselves more for their external abilities and appearances when compared to those with higher socioeconomic status (Dellasega & Nixon, 2003).

Researchers have found that it is those communities, such as the middle class, that have unyielding expectations regarding gender roles that encourage a pandemic of relational aggression (Simmons, 2002). Communities that value open conflict and assertiveness skills may be less likely to facilitate relational aggression (Simmons, 2002). Dellasega and Nixon (2003) stated that girls must be taught that various qualities make an individual unique, and solely concentrating on external attributes can reinforce the idea that appearances comprise a girl's identity.

Relational aggression has been further defined to manifest within two separate distinctions. Similar to the types of aggression defined in boys, The Ophelia Project (2005) defines relational aggression as being either proactive or reactive in nature. Proactive aggression is seen as instrumental relational aggression that one intentionally uses as a means to obtain something, such as spreading a rumor due to being jealous about one's popularity (The Ophelia Project, 2005). Reactive aggression, on the other hand, is seen as a means to seek revenge for an act committed by the aggressor upon the victim, such as spreading a rumor in response to being isolated during lunch (The Ophelia Project, 2005).

In order to avoid the adverse effects associated with relational aggression, there is a need to intervene when relational aggression occurs. Research has suggested relational aggression to be a risk factor that may increase the chance for such individuals to become lonely, feel more isolated than nonaggressive children, be less accepted by their peers, and have a greater disposition towards internalizing disorders such as depression and withdrawal (Crick & Grotpeter, 1995), social avoidance, and anxiety (Crick & Grotpeter, 1996). Victims of relationally aggressive acts have also been found to report an increase in negative attitudes about social situations with others (Phelps, 2001) and are often assigned to the role of victim initially and continually throughout elementary school (Crick & Grotpeter, 1996). In addition, girls with relationally aggressive characteristics may be more likely to perceive themselves as having a lower sense of self-esteem (Prinstein et al., 2001). Adaptive social-psychological adjustment has also been indicated to be affected by relational aggression (Crick & Grotpeter, 1995). According to researchers, negative outcomes are likely to be encountered by both the aggressors and targets of relational aggression (McKay, 2003).

The implications of these findings are significant. If left untreated and ignored, such problems may be likely to influence underachievement while jeopardizing success in school. Victims of relational aggression may come to view school as an unwelcoming place that only increases the intense social isolation that they feel (Skowronksi et al., 2005). Unattended relational aggression can also become reinforcing for individuals to use, as they see it as a means to get power while keeping high status within peer groups (Skowronksi et al., 2005). Educators, as well as parents, who do not intervene when relational aggression occurs often reinforce the message that such behaviors are normative for girls, and may give the impression that children grow out of such deviant behaviors (Yoon et al., 2004).

Research does not support the idea that aggressive individuals are likely to grow out of such behaviors. Relational aggression has been found to present at a very young age and can remain stable and persist into adulthood if left untreated early on (The Ophelia Project, 2005; Crick, Casas, & Ku, 1999). Engagement in relational aggression has been found to be a stable occurrence that often derives out of learned behavior, as many adult women can be found to exhibit relationally aggressive behaviors (Dellasega & Nixon, 2003; Simmons, 2002; The Ophelia Project, 2005).

Such learned behaviors early on can become frameworks or guidelines for how to treat others in adolescent and adult relationships later in life (The Ophelia Project; Wiseman, 2002). When relational aggression is disregarded, girls can come to believe that this behavior is an expected way to interact with others and is preparation for establishing relationships with adults (Simmons, 2002). Unresolved difficulties associated with relational aggression that continue into adulthood may be responsible for creating a lowered sense of self-esteem, confidence, and wholeness that can lead to unresolved problems (Pipher, 1994).

Intervention for Relational Aggression — Belief Systems

If beliefs regarding relational aggression are seen as instrumental in increasing one's popularity and sense of belonging, it is likely that belief systems are also influential in the participation and maintenance of relational aggression. Therefore, participation in discussions and working to change relational aggression beliefs and behaviors within peer groups will help to decrease the negativity that relational difficulties play in relationships (Brown et al., 1999). Dellasega and Nixon (2003) have agreed that changing normative belief systems about relational aggression is an effective way to change expectations of acceptable behaviors for girls. As the research indicates, relational aggression has often gone undetected by adults because of its covert nature. It is reasonable, therefore, to expect that such behaviors might be considered normal, acceptable behavior for girls to engage in unless they are taught otherwise. Individuals may often ignore such behaviors as being characteristic of bullying and may see them as interrelated components of friendships (Simmons, 2002). Therefore, girls need to understand and be taught the difference between emotionally healthy relationships and abusive, bullying relations with others. Pipher (1994) further indicates that girls need to understand that a difference in thinking and feeling about things exists. It is important that individuals must be able to distinguish between emotional reasoning and thinking when making decisions about important issues such as friendships (Pipher, 1994).

According to a study conducted by The Ophelia Project, beliefs about relational aggression were likely to affect the participation in aggressive behaviors in a group of middle school girls (Nixon, 2005). This study designed a curriculum that sought to alter previously held ideas about relational aggression by challenging belief systems to change participation in relational aggression (Nixon, 2005). Adolescents who believed that relationally aggressive behaviors, such as excluding others and spreading rumors, were appropriate and normative exhibited a greater likelihood for being aggressors of relational aggression (Nixon, 2005).

According to the study conducted by The Ophelia Project, girls who believe that relational aggression is acceptable are more likely to engage in such behaviors (Nixon, 2005). Healthy girls realize the importance for establishing and adhering to personal values that will not be compromised in order to fit into the culture to be popular (Pipher, 1994). Addressing relational aggression when it occurs, such as telling girls these behaviors are unacceptable, is likely to decrease the involvement in relational aggression. Consistent rules about acceptable behaviors need to be reinforced to girls (Dellasega & Nixon, 2003). It needs to be made clear to girls that hurting others is always unacceptable (Dellasega & Nixon, 2003). Educators, as well as parents, have an important role in intervening with such behaviors when they occur, as they are likely to decrease the involvement in relationally aggressive behaviors when they set specific guidelines and expectations for appropriate behaviors for girls. Addressing such issues when they occur also helps girls to be accountable for their actions. Girls may be less likely to possess the motivation and maturity to refrain from engaging in relational aggression without the assistance from others (Dellasega & Nixon, 2003).

Intervention for Relational Aggression — Assertiveness Skills

Changing belief systems about relational aggression is not sufficient enough to produce change. Girls need to be taught effective strategies for dealing with their aggressor and situations involving relational aggression. One of the most efficient ways to deal with relational aggression is through direct confrontation, one that allows victims and aggressors the opportunity to address discerning situations by talking about the ways in which they were hurt by others (Skowronski et al., 2005).

One way to give girls the tools for dealing with such difficult situations is to help them develop assertiveness skills. Girls need to be taught the definition of aggressiveness versus assertiveness. Assertiveness skills seek to express one's feelings, rights, and opinions in a way that does not hurt others; whereas, aggressiveness seeks to meet one's needs without thinking about the effects it will have on others (Dellasega & Nixon, 2003). Strategies for engaging in assertiveness skills include confirming others' feelings or actions, stating ones' feelings about the situation, and asking the person to change their hurtful behavior (Dellasega & Nixon, 2003). Dellasega and Nixon (2003) recommend that girls address difficult issues by first stating a positive, followed by telling the aggressor to cease the aversive behavior, while completing the discussion with yet another positive statement. Victims who are able to tell their aggressor about their feelings may be seen as courageous and may therefore be perceived as being less willing to be the victim of aggressive acts (Skowronski, 2005).

Aside from learning what aggressiveness and assertiveness means, girls also need to be taught about passivity and the effects that may occur from doing nothing when relational aggression happens. Girls need to be taught that passive actions are void of taking action, and this behavior sends the implicit message that aggression is acceptable (Dellasega & Nixon, 2003). In order for girls to be responsible for their behaviors, as well as for their lives, they must be taught to make choices consciously and carefully (Pipher, 1994). They must recognize that making decisions is a personal responsibility that must be done among the many influences of peers and culture (Pipher, 1994).

Girls must define the values and boundaries for their relationships and work toward having relations with others that are consistent with their standards (Pipher, 1994). Girls must be given opportunities to role play situations involving relational aggression in order to feel empowered and be confident in dealing with such events when they occur (Dellasega & Nixon, 2003).

Intervention for Relational Aggression — Confidence and Active Involvement

Girls need to believe in themselves and their abilities (Dellasega & Nixon, 2003) while looking toward themselves versus extrinsic reinforcers for validation (Pipher, 1994). A healthy sense of self-esteem is often developed when girls are engaged in activities that make them feel confident (Dellasega & Nixon, 2003) and allow themselves the opportunity to be individuals who fit into many roles, such as athlete or an activist, while resisting the unrealistic role of femininity (Pipher, 1994). Girls should be encouraged to seek out things that allow them to obtain confidence, learn to show empathy for others, and be supportive and kind towards one another (Dellasega & Nixon, 2003). Activities that allow girls to feel accomplished about contributions they have made, whether it be through things such as participation in volunteer work or being involved in political activities, will enable girls the opportunity to become more concerned about things other than themselves (Piper, 1994). Girls who have passions, or interests that go beyond themselves, have protective factors that they can revert to when difficulties arise (Pipher, 1994).

In order to help promote supportive attitudes towards others and change perspectives of aggressive behavior, girls need to be engaged in activities that build upon teamwork and cooperation, such as volunteering or developing group projects (Dellasega & Nixon, 2003). Girls should also be encouraged to develop adaptive coping skills, such as writing in a journal or exercising, in order to help cope with relational aggression (Dellasega & Nixon, 2003). When girls are allowed the opportunity to embrace their true selves, or explore various possibilities for their lives, and are encouraged to treat others with respect, girls are more likely to resist negative symptoms related to pathology (Pipher, 1994).

Girls who remain actively involved with their families also have protective factors to buffer against negative outcomes. According to Pipher (1994), girls who have a positive sense of self keep ties with family members and have a sense of loyalty to them even during difficult times. Being involved in the community and feeling connected to a positive adult role model is one important way to facilitate mental health and an overall sense of security (Debold et al., 1999). Girls must be allowed the chance to become individuals, but socially and emotionally healthy girls are cognizant in the way they are loved and connected to their family (Pipher, 1994).

Intervention for Relational Aggression — A School-Based Program

Empirically or evidence based programs that are built upon research literature have shown impressive evidence for behavioral change as can be seen through the research of Merrell and his colleagues. Merrell and colleagues (2004) have noted specifically that when scientific guidelines are adhered to in the literature mental health, emotional, social, and behavioral problems can be prevented and remediated to a significant degree. Social and emotional learning are essential tools that all children must receive in order to be better prepared to meet the demands of an ever-changing society today. Social and emotional learning has become increasingly important in education, as it has often been linked as an essential component to obtaining academic achievement (Merrell, Juskelis, & Tran, 2004). Research continues to demonstrate how emotion is essential in the process of learning (Gewertz, 2003). Social and emotional programs that teach students how to effectively deal with the stress that interferes with effective learning have suggested that the brain's functioning, as well as academic achievement, is enhanced when these programs are taught to students (Gewertz, 2003).

The present social and emotional curriculum intends to teach students the emotional skills and strategies they need in order to deal with the stress that can be caused by relational aggression. The foundation of the present curriculum has been developed according to both relational aggression research as well as the social and emotional literature. Results from initial studies conducted on this program have shown promising results. A moderate to high percentage of individuals who have received this curriculum have shown gains in their knowledge and beliefs of relational aggression. Relational aggression is a topic that is too important to be ignored.

When left ignored and untreated, relational aggression is likely to increase the spreading of relationally aggressive behaviors and be considered normative behavior for girls (Nixon, 2005). As evidenced by Nixon (2005), girls who are explicitly taught to change their belief systems about relational aggression are more likely to perceive this type of aggression as being intolerable. Girls must first understand that relational aggression is bullying behavior that hurts others (Dellasega & Nixon, 2003). The present curriculum explicitly teaches awareness about relational aggression while teaching girls to alter their belief systems and change negative thinking into more proactive, assertive thinking. The curriculum asks girls to evaluate and monitor how they treat others, while teaching them how to take responsibility for their actions.

Research has indicated that engagement in relational aggression is likely to increase maladaptive perceptions in self-esteem (Prinstein et al., 2001), children are more prone to feel lonely and isolated from others while being less accepted (Crick & Grotpeter, 1995), and demonstrate more pessimistic attitudes about social situations (Phelps, 2001). Accordingly, socio-emotional curriculums give such individuals the skills to become active problem solvers who are able to communicate effectively with others through the teaching of active listening and assertiveness skills (Merrell et al., 2004). It is expected that such curriculums have the potential to be effective in the prevention of relational aggression as well. It is expected that a program specifically developed for treating issues related to relational aggression will provide individuals with the tools necessary to deal more proactively with others when female bullying occurs. This curriculum teaches girls to evaluate their perceptions about themselves and to decide how they want to be viewed by others. It has girls examine if their actions match their perceptions of who they want to be. In addition, girls are taught how to use problem solving and assertiveness skills to solve situations involving relational aggression.

In order to prevent relational aggression, girls must be taught how it is unacceptable behavior. Relational aggression, or female bullying, must be explicitly challenged and confronted if it is to cease. Girls need to be taught how engagement in relational aggression is likely to facilitate negative outcomes for all individuals involved. Collectively, girls must agree to reject relational aggression in order to prevent the emotional distress that it can cause.

SESSION ONE:
General Objectives and Goals

Purpose and Group Objectives

- Girls will identify acceptable girl behaviors.
- Girls will learn to appreciate their unique abilities.
- Girls will learn to appreciate the unique abilities of others.
- Girls will demonstrate their current knowledge of relational aggression.

Confidentiality

Discuss the need for group confidentiality. Some reasons may include building trust and security in the group so that all girls feel that they can participate. Some of the topics discussed may be sensitive subjects for girls in the group, and everyone needs to feel that they are safe to contribute.

Mandatory Reporting

Explain mandatory reporting procedures. Confidentiality is broken when someone expresses the desire to hurt themself or another person. Such intent needs to be reported to another adult in order to ensure that all individuals are safe.

Activity 1.1: Establishing Group Rules

Overview: The girls will establish 3-5 positively stated group rules. Have the group participate in coming up with the rules for the group. Girls will understand the importance of following these rules in order for all group members to feel comfortable participating.

Objectives: Develop rules that all group members agree to follow. Rules may include:
- Be respectful of everyone in the group.
- Keep all discussions in the group private.
- Be prepared for group by completing homework.

Procedures:
- List the group rules on an overhead or dry erase board, and have the girls copy the rules on the Activity 1.1 reproducible page found in Appendix A.
- Have the girls sign one form and distribute a copy for each girl.

Activity 1.2: Group Building Exercise

Overview: Group members will develop a sense of group unity by examining the similarities and differences that they share with others in the group. Girls will also begin to understand the differences in others.

Objectives:
- Girls will identify some benefits to being similar to others.
- Girls will identify some benefits to being unique and different from others.

- Girls will learn something new about someone from the group.
- The girls will begin to appreciate the differences in others.

Procedures:
- Using reproducible handout 1.2 in Appendix A, have the girls agree upon two of their favorite categories and two future categories that they would like to write about (i.e. Future Goal or Future Career, etc.).
- Have them write these four categories in the appropriate space on their handout.
- Separate the girls into small groups to share their answers. While they are sharing, have the girls write in what they found to be similar to and different from others.

Discussion Questions:
1. Were there similar responses in the group? What were the similar responses?
2. Were there any different responses in the group? What were the different responses?
3. Was there anything that surprised you about someone else's response? Why?

Discussion Points:
- Emphasize similarities among the group to promote a sense of unity, while emphasizing differences in order to promote acceptance among the group.
- Being similar to someone else, or sharing something with that person, may be a benefit because great friendships may develop due to shared interests.
- Being different or unique from someone else might be beneficial, because it may mean that you have something unique to contribute to a friendship.

Activity 1.3: Relational Aggression Assessment Measure

Overview: Girls will demonstrate their current knowledge and belief systems about relational aggression.

Objectives:
- Girls will demonstrate their current knowledge of relational aggression prior to implementation of the relational aggression curriculum.
- Girls will demonstrate what their current belief systems about relational aggression are prior to implementation of the relational aggression curriculum.

Procedures:
- Copy and hand out the Relational Aggression Assessment Measure located in Appendix B.
- Explain to the girls that this quiz will evaluate what they currently know and believe about relational aggression.
- Explain that their answers will be kept confidential.

Activity 1.4: What Do I Want to Know

Overview: Girls will activate prior background knowledge about relational aggression by organizing and listing the facts they currently know about relational aggression, as well as if they believe it is okay to be relationally aggressive towards others. Girls will also list what they want to learn about relational aggression during the group sessions.

Objectives:
- Girls will list the current facts or knowledge they have about relational aggression.
- Girls will think about and list what they want to learn about relational aggression.

Procedures:
- Have the girls complete reproducible Activity 1.4 located in Appendix A by filling in their answers next to the lines provided on this handout.
- Complete the top portion of this activity. The bottom portion will be used during a later session. You may want to collect these worksheets, as the girls will need them again for session five.

Activity 1.5: **Homework — Relational Aggression**

Overview: The girls will reflect and generalize the information learned from the group sessions by completing homework lessons due at the next week's session.

Objectives:
- Girls will think and reflect about what relational aggression is.
- Girls will use their prior background knowledge about relational aggression to complete this activity.

Procedures:
- Copy and hand out reproducible Activity 1.5: Homework located in Appendix A to the girls.
- Have them complete this activity and bring it with them to next week's group session.
- Discuss and review this activity prior to beginning the objectives for session two.

Discussion Questions: (for discussion at the beginning of next week's session)
1. What is relational aggression?
2. What does relational aggression look like?
3. How does relational aggression hurt others?

In order to increase completion of the homework activities and increase participation, an optional point system may be developed using one of the following options:

Option 1: develop a group point total that girls will strive to reach by the last session. Points are earned when everyone has their homework completed for the designated week.

Option 2: provide random individual reinforcement for the completion of their homework each week.

Leader Notes for Group Session One

Date: _____

Time: _____

Girls Present:

_____

_____

Girls Absent:

_____

_____

Summary of Session One:

_____

_____

_____

What went well:

_____

_____

_____

What did not go well and may need improvement:

_____

_____

_____

Important notes:

_____

_____

_____

_____

SESSION TWO:
Relational Aggression Defined

Purpose and Group Objectives

- Girls will identify what relational aggression is and looks like.
- Girls will understand how relational aggression hurts others.
- Girls will learn to empathize with victims of relational aggression.
- Girls will learn strategies for relational aggression.

Review last week's lesson by going over any concerns or questions and summarize last week's objectives. Choose one participant to give a brief summary from last week. Review the homework assignment for this week. If using the optional point system, award points for homework completion and add to the group's total points. Review and post group rules from last week's session.

Activity 2.1: Mean Girl Behaviors

Overview: Girls will be able to define what relational aggression is. Girls will identify that relational aggression is also known as female bullying.

Objectives:

- Girls will list and provide characteristics and examples of relational aggression.
- Girls will learn that relational aggression is an imbalance of power.
- The girls will understand that relational aggression is using friendships to hurt others.
- Girls will learn that relational aggression is repetitive, controlling behavior.

Procedures:

- Hand out reproducible Activity 2.1 in Appendix A.
- Use the following discussion questions and points to engage the girls in a conversation about relational aggression.
- Have the girls list the ways that they have seen girls be mean to other girls by writing the ways on this worksheet.

Discussion Questions:

1. What is relational aggression?
2. What does relational aggression look like?

Discussion Points:

- Relational aggression is an imbalance of power when one person uses friendships or relationships to hurt others.
- Relational aggression, also known as female bullying, is repetitive behavior that someone uses in order to control another person.
- Examples of relational aggression include: gossiping about others, talking about someone behind their back, using body language in a hurtful way (i.e. eye rolling, turning your back on someone when they are talking), excluding others, telling someone not to be friends with certain people, and cyber bullying

Activity 2.2: **Mean Girls in Action — Movie Clip**

Overview: Girls will define what relational aggression is. Girls will observe how relational aggression hurts others when given a visual example.

Objectives:
- Girls will be able to list examples of relational aggression.
- Girls will understand how relational aggression hurts others.
- Girls will understand that relational aggression hurts oneself.

Procedures:
- Copy and hand out reproducible Activity 2.2 from Appendix A to each girl.
- Watch a movie clip depicting relational aggression in action (sample movies might include: *Odd Girl Out, She's All That, 10 Things I Hate About You, Mean Girls*).
- Have the girls complete this worksheet by writing in the relationally aggressive behaviors they saw from watching the movie clip. The discussion questions below can be used to facilitate a discussion.

Discussion Questions:
1. What mean behaviors (i.e. relationally aggressive behaviors) were observed?
2. Who was the aggressor in the movie clip?
   - What did the aggressor do?
   - How did the aggressor feel?
   - Did this behavior hurt her in some way?
   - Did the aggressor get what she wanted by acting this way?
3. Who was the victim in the movie clip?
   - What did the victim do?
   - How did the victim feel?
   - How did the aggressor's behavior hurt her?

Activity 2.3: **Relational Aggression Book Study**

Overview: The girls will learn to empathize with others who have faced similar situations involving relational aggression through a book study.

Objectives:
- Girls will understand what relational aggression or female bullying is.
- Girls will learn to empathize with girls who are victims of relational aggression.
- Girls will learn to take the perspective of others.
- Girls will understand that relational aggression hurts both the aggressors and victims.

Procedures:
- Read a passage from a book depicting a scenario of relational aggression. An option might be to hand out the same book to all girls and use this book throughout the sessions. See Appendix E for a list of sample books and passage selections.
- Have the girls complete the Activity 2.3 discussion questions worksheet found in Appendix A.

Discussion Questions:

1. What was the mean behavior or relationally aggressive act observed?
2. Who was the victim in this passage? Who was the aggressor?
3. What did the victim do in this passage (i.e. were any strategies observed)?
4. What did the aggressor do in this passage?
5. Who was hurt in this passage? How were they hurt?
6. Describe any positive strategies that were used in this passage.

Discussion Points:

■ It is important during this discussion to explain that relational aggression hurts both the victim and the aggressor.
■ Relational aggression may lead to problems later in life if issues are left ignored and not talked about, such as depression (i.e. feeling severely sad for an extended period of time), anxiety (i.e. worrying about things constantly or being afraid of coming to school), and withdrawal from friends (i.e. wanting to be alone and away from people). Explain to the girls that these are extreme feelings that need to be addressed with an adult.
■ Relational aggression can start at a young age (i.e. children as young as preschool engage in relational aggression) and is unacceptable behavior for both girls and boys.

Activity 2.4: Role Playing and Active Learning

Overview: Girls will be able to make a connection between relational aggression and a personal experience they have had with relational aggression. Girls will begin to identify specific strategies for relational aggression.

Objectives:

■ Girls will list personal experiences they have had with relational aggression or develop a scenario depicting relational aggression.
■ Girls will share their experiences with others.
■ Girls will learn to be empathetic of others.
■ Girls will brainstorm strategies to use given their situations or experiences.

Procedures:

■ Reproduce Activity 2.4: Role Playing and Active Learning in Appendix A, and have the girls write about a personal experience they have had with relational aggression. Or, have the girls create a possible scenario of relational aggression.
■ Separate girls into small groups, and have them share their responses with others.
■ After they have shared their experiences, have the girls brainstorm different strategies that they could use in each of their situations or scenarios.

Discussion Questions:

1. Could the girls relate to someone else in the group? Were they able to be empathetic?
2. Was it easy to share their personal experiences in the group? Why or why not?
3. What were some strategies that the girls discussed given their situation or experience?

Activity 2.5: **Question Cards — Relational Aggression**

Overview: Girls will demonstrate what they know about relational aggression. Girls will gain a better understanding of what relational aggression is.

Objectives:
- Girls will gain a better understanding of relational aggression or female bullying.
- Girls will identify what they still need to learn about relational aggression.

Procedures:
- Hand out an index card to each group member, and have them write down one question they want clarified about relational aggression from this week's session. Or, have the girls write one thing they learned about relational aggression from this week.
- Collect these cards as the girls leave.
- Review these cards and discuss them prior to beginning session three's objectives.

Discussion Questions: (for discussion at the beginning of next week's session)
1. Were there any questions about relational aggression that need clarification?
2. Review a few key points or statements that were listed about relational aggression.

Activity 2.6: **Homework — Cliques**

Overview: The girls will generalize the information learned from the group session by completing homework for next week's session.

Objectives:
- Girls will become aware of their thoughts and feelings about girl groups.
- Girls will become aware of girl groups and the roles girls play in these groups.

Procedures:
- Reproduce Activity 2.6: Homework in Appendix A for this activity.
- Hand out a copy of this worksheet to each girl, and have them complete this worksheet for next week's group session.
- Explain that these questions will be discussed next week.
- If using the point option, explain that the girls can earn points for bringing back their completed homework next week.

Discussion Questions: (for discussion at the beginning of next week's session)
1. Are there girl groups or cliques that exist in your school?
2. If so, do girls play certain roles in these girl groups?
3. What roles are there in girl groups or cliques?
4. What do you think is the reason girls play the roles?

Leader Notes for Group Session Two

Date: _____

Time: _____

Girls Present:

_____

_____

Girls Absent:

_____

_____

Summary of Session Two:

_____

_____

_____

What went well:

_____

_____

_____

What did not go well and may need improvement:

_____

_____

_____

Important notes:

_____

_____

_____

_____

S E S S I O N   T H R E E :
Cliques, Girl Groups, and Popularity

Purpose and Group Objectives

- Girls will learn to work cooperatively with one another.
- Girls will identify what a clique is.
- Girls will identify how clique behavior relates to relational aggression.
- Girls will identify the influences that friendship groups can have.

Review last week's lesson by going over any concerns or questions and summarize last week's objectives. Choose one participant to give a brief summary from last week. Review the homework assignment for this week. If using the optional point system, award points for homework completion and add to the group's total points. Review and post group rules.

P A R T   1

Activity 3.1: Group Project

Overview: The girls will understand what relational aggression or female bullying is. Girls will learn to use problem solving and cooperative strategies for working with others in order to demonstrate their knowledge about relational aggression.

Objectives:
- Girls will demonstrate that they understand what relational aggression is.
- Girls will demonstrate strategies for treating relational aggression.
- Girls will learn to work cooperatively with one another in a small group format.
- Girls will learn to use problem solving skills.

Procedures:
- Separate girls into groups of two or three, preferably with others they usually do not work with.
- Explain that the girls will need to develop and present a way to approach relational aggression.
- They will need to present their ideas to the group during the last group session.
- *Extension Activity:* Have the girls present their ideas to other classrooms in order to increase awareness about relational aggression.
  - Sample ideas may include: a play about relational aggression/female bullying, making a poster or collage about healthy relationships, designing an after school club for girls, creating a game about relational aggression, power point presentation, newsletter, brochure, crossword puzzle, role play activities, or a book about relational aggression

Activity 3.2: Clique Behaviors

Overview: Girls will increase their awareness of relationally aggressive behaviors that can be found in cliques. Girls will identify if they are part of a clique and are relationally aggressive towards others.

Objectives:
- Girls will be able to define what a clique or girl group is.
- Girls will make a connection between relational aggression and clique behaviors.
- Girls will identify if they are relationally aggressive towards others.
- Girls will learn to respect and appreciate the rights of others.

Procedures:
- Copy and hand out Activity 3.2: Clique Behaviors in Appendix A.
- Have the girls choose the option that represents what they think about girl groups.
- Facilitate a discussion about cliques using the discussion questions and points below.
- After the discussion, have the girls complete the last question on their worksheet.

Discussion Questions:
1. What are cliques?
2. What do cliques look like?
3. Do cliques have certain rules?
4. Do cliques have influence over friendships and what people do?
5. Is it bad to be part of a clique or girl group?

Discussion Points:
- Cliques are exclusive or selective groups of girls that may want only certain people to be a part of their group.
- There can be specific roles in cliques, and girls who don't fit into the group can be excluded and made fun of for being different from the cliques' rules.
- Cliques can have specific standards in order to be accepted into their group.
- These rules or standards can influence what someone does, as people can become dependent on each other and may be less likely to consider their own thoughts or seek adult help when there is a problem.
- Reinforce that it is not bad to be part of a group in general. Everyone is not expected to be friends with everyone. However, everyone is expected to respect the rights of each other. When girl groups exclude, gossip, or hurt others they are not respecting the rights of others. This is unacceptable clique behavior, because these girls are acting like bullies.

Activity 3.3: Influence of Friendship Groups

Overview: Girls will understand how friendship groups can influence the choices that one makes. Girls will learn to make choices based on their own thoughts and feelings.

Objectives:
- Girls will learn to identify how their friends may influence their behaviors and choices.
- Girls will learn to make choices that are based on their own thoughts.
- Girls will begin to understand how their thinking influences their behavior.
- Girls will identify how easy it is for them to be relationally aggressive towards others while in their friendship groups.

Procedures:

■ Discuss how friendship groups influence the idea of appearances, thoughts, and behaviors using reproducible Activity 3.3 Influence of Friendship Groups found in Appendix A. The discussion questions and points below can be used to facilitate a discussion.

■ Have the girls complete this activity by circling yes or no depending on the experiences they have had with their friendship groups.

■ Have them answer the question at the bottom of this page in order to determine if their thoughts and beliefs are consistent with the beliefs of their friendship group.

Discussion Questions:

1. Do friendship groups influence how someone tries to dress?
2. Do friendship groups influence how someone tries to act?
3. Do friendship groups influence how someone thinks about something?
4. Is there pressure from your group of friends to be or act a certain way?
5. Do friendship groups make it okay to gossip about or exclude others if the group feels it is acceptable behavior?
6. Do friends in the group get angry or jealous if someone wants to hang out with someone outside of the group?
7. Do girls believe that being in the popular group protects someone from being gossiped about?
8. Do you exclude others to be in the popular group?

Discussion Points:

■ Reiterate that being in the popular group does not protect one from being bullied, including being gossiped or talked about.

■ Girls who are in the popular group can also bully and use relational aggression against others.

■ When you repetitively exclude, ignore others on purpose, or gossip about others to be in a popular group you are acting like a bully.

■ Being popular is not a bad thing, except when it becomes an acceptable way according to the group to hurt others.

Activity 3.4: Role Play Scenarios

Overview: Girls will learn how to celebrate the accomplishments of others, develop confidence in their abilities, and learn strategies for relational aggression.

Objectives:

■ Girls will learn to celebrate the accomplishments of others.
■ Girls will develop and practice self-confidence skills.
■ Girls will be able to take action given a relational aggression situation.

Procedures:

■ Separate girls into small groups and hand out a situation card to each group. The scenarios are included in Appendix A. You may want to cut and paste each situation on card stock or an index card.

■ Have the girls read each of their scenarios in their groups.

■ Have the girls complete the questions for Activity 3.4 in Appendix A by writing their responses to the questions on the space provided.

- After the girls have completed answering the questions, have each group read their scenario and discuss their responses as a whole group.

Discussion Questions:

1. How did each group choose to handle this situation? What would they say?
2. How did each group show self-confidence while still appreciating and respecting the other person's feelings?
3. How did girls in the group avoid becoming relationally aggressive? How did they decide to prevent relational aggression from happening in each of their situations?

Activity 3.5: Girl Group Roles

Overview: Girls will understand the different roles that girls play in cliques or girl groups, how each role can be problematic, and how to intervene or deal with each role.

Objectives:
- The girls will understand what the different roles in girl groups are.
- Girls will identify the problems that may occur from playing a certain role in a clique.
- The girls will develop and practice strategies for coping with each role in a clique.

Procedures:
- Reproduce and hand out Activity 3.5 Girl Group Roles in Appendix A to the girls.
- Lead the girls in a discussion about the different roles in cliques using the leader's guide located in Appendix A.
- Have the girls fill in the blanks on their worksheets while using the discussion questions.

Discussion Questions:
1. What roles are there in girl groups? Who plays what role?
2. What does each role look like? How is it different from each role?
3. What are potential problems in each of the roles?

Discussion Points:
- There are various roles in girl groups or cliques, such as the group leader, girl in the middle, the victims, and the bystanders.
- The group leader may always want to make choices for everyone. This person may want power and control and is not afraid to intimidate others. The girl in the middle may use information in order to cause problems in or outside the group. The victim may feel isolated and excluded from others and may feel helpless. The bystanders may not know what to do and feel caught.
- The group leader may not understand how to have healthy relationships with others. People may not trust the girl in the middle to be honest and truthful. The victim may learn to become anxious and afraid to make relationships with others. The bystanders may not know what they want.

Activity 3.6: Relational Aggression Book Study

Overview: The girls will learn to empathize with others who have faced similar situations involving relational aggression through a book study.

Objectives:
- Girls will understand what relational aggression or female bullying is.
- Girls will learn to empathize with girls who are victims of relational aggression.
- Girls will learn to take the perspective of others.
- Girls will understand that relational aggression hurts both the aggressors and victims.

Procedures:
- Read a passage from a book depicting relational aggression. See Appendix E for a list of sample books and passage selections.
- Complete the following discussion questions by having the girls write their answers to the discussion questions on the reproducible Activity 3.6: Relational Aggression Book Study worksheet found in Appendix A.

Discussion Questions:
1. What was the mean behavior or relationally aggressive act observed?
2. Who was the victim in this passage? Who was the aggressor?
3. What did the victim do in this passage (i.e. were any strategies observed)?
4. What did the aggressor do in this passage?
5. Who was hurt in this passage? How were they hurt?
6. Describe any positive strategies that were used in this passage.

PART 2

Activity 3.7: Assertiveness Skills

Overview: Girls will be able to define relational aggression and identify what the negative and positive strategies are for relational aggression. Girls will specifically identify what assertiveness skills are and will learn how to apply them in real life situations.

Objectives:
- Girls will identify what it means to be relationally aggressive, passive, and assertive.
- The girls will learn what assertiveness skills are.
- Girls will practice using assertiveness skills.
- Girls will learn how to apply assertiveness strategies to real life situations.

Procedures:
- Have the girls refer to Activity 3.7: Assertiveness Skills in Appendix A in order to be able to define relational aggression, passivity, and assertiveness skills.
- Have the girls practice using assertiveness skills by using the sample script on this worksheet.
- Separate the girls into small groups, and have them role play what they could say to someone who is bullying them.

Discussion Questions:
1. How do you know if someone is being relationally aggressive? What does it look like?
2. What does being passive mean? Is it effective in treating relational aggression?

3. What are assertiveness skills? Are they effective in treating relational aggression?
4. What is the ACT strategy?
5. What problems with relational aggression are currently happening to you? What are the possible choices to handle each of these situations? What could you say and do?

    A = *Acknowledge* the friendship and the person.

    C = *Change* the situation by telling the person what you want to be different.

    T = *Together* come up with a solution that benefits both people.

Activity 3.8: Assertiveness Skills Practice

Overview: Girls will be able to practice using assertiveness skills, while being able to apply these strategies to real life situations. Girls will also learn how to use problem solving strategies when relational aggression occurs.

Objectives:

- Girls will develop their problem solving skills.
  - Identify what the problem or relationally aggressive situation is.
  - Brainstorm any and all possible choices to solve this problem, including the use of assertiveness skills.
- Girls will learn how to use assertiveness skills in real life situations.
  - Act out or role play how you would implement this choice in real life.

Procedures:

- Have the girls refer to Activity 3.8: Assertiveness Skills Practice in Appendix A to complete this activity.
- Have the girls use their problem solving skills by writing a current problem they are facing with relational aggression, what choices there are to solve this problem, and how the choice would look in real life if they acted it out in the appropriate column on this worksheet.
- Separate the girls into small groups, and have them role play what they could say or do to someone who is bullying them.

Activity 3.9: Behavior Contract or Promise

Overview: Girls will be able to identify another strategy for dealing with relational aggression. Girls will identify acceptable and unacceptable friendship behaviors.

Objectives:

- Girls will identify what a contract or promise is.
- Girls will set standards for acceptable and unacceptable behaviors.
- Unacceptable behaviors = any behavior that intentionally hurts others, including relationally aggressive behaviors (i.e. exclusion, isolation, gossip, cyber bullying)
- Acceptable behaviors = behaviors that benefit everyone in a group (i.e. including others, talking respectfully towards others, talking out our problems when mad)

Procedures:

- A sample contract or promise is included in Appendix A. After reviewing the sample contract, have the girls create their own contracts or promises using Activity 3.9 in Appendix A.

- Have the girls define the following objectives in their contracts:
  - Unacceptable / Acceptable Friendship Behaviors
  - The Problem or Behavior to Change
  - The Friendship Promise (that everyone has agreed to uphold and follow)
  - People Involved
  - The Action Plan
  - Importance of the Contract or Promise

Activity 3.10: Clique Action

Overview: Girls will be able to identify certain roles in cliques or girl groups, while identifying the specific strategies for dealing with each role. Girls will learn to apply the strategies they have learned throughout the group sessions.

Objectives:
- Girls will identify specific roles in cliques or girl groups.
- Girls will identify specific strategies for each role.
- Girls will demonstrate that they can apply strategies learned throughout this group to real life situations involving relational aggression.

Procedures:
- Reproduce Activity 3.10 found in Appendix A. Using the discussion questions below and the leader's guide located in Appendix A, have the girls fill in the appropriate blanks.
- Lead the girls in a discussion about different strategies that each role could use when relational aggression happens.

Discussion Questions:
1. What strategies could the group leader use?
2. What strategies could the girl in the middle use?
3. What strategies could the victim use?
4. What strategies could the bystanders use?

Activity 3.11: Question Cards — Clique Behaviors

Overview: Girls will demonstrate what they know about cliques. Girls will demonstrate strategies for clique behaviors.

Objectives:
- Girls will understand cliques and clique behavior.
- Girls will understand how cliques relate to relational aggression.

Procedures:
- Hand out an index card to each group member, and have them write down one question they want clarified about cliques from this week's session. Or, have the girls write one thing they learned about cliques and relational aggression.
- Collect these cards as the girls leave.

■ Review these cards and discuss them prior to beginning session four's objectives.

Discussion Questions: (for discussion at the beginning of next week's session)
1. Were there any questions about cliques that need clarification?
2. Review a few key points or statements that were listed about cliques.

Activity 3.12: Homework — Popularity

Overview: The girls will generalize the information learned from the group session by completing homework for next week's session.

Objectives:
■ Girls will think about what popularity means to them.
■ Girls will identify advantages and disadvantages of being popular.
■ Girls will determine if they want to be popular.
■ The girls will evaluate what they are willing to do in order to fit in or be popular.

Procedures:
■ Reproduce Activity 3.12: Homework in Appendix A for this activity.
■ Hand out a copy of this worksheet to each girl, and have them complete this worksheet for next week's group session.
■ Explain that these questions will be discussed next week.
■ If using the point option, explain that girls can earn points for bringing back their completed homework next week.

Discussion Questions: (for discussion at the beginning of next week's session)
1. What does being popular mean (i.e. definitions and what does it look like)?
2. What are some advantages and disadvantages of being popular?
3. Is popularity something you want?
4. What are you willing to do in order to be popular?

Leader Notes for Group Session Three

Date: _____

Time: _____

Girls Present:

_____

_____

Girls Absent:

_____

_____

Summary of Session Three:

_____

_____

_____

What went well:

_____

_____

What did not go well and may need improvement:

_____

_____

_____

Important notes:

_____

_____

_____

SESSION FOUR:
Developing Healthy Friendships

Purpose and Group Objectives
■ Girls will evaluate what they value in a friendship.
■ Girls will identify what a healthy friendship is and looks like.
■ Girls will use problem solving skills.
■ Girls will monitor and evaluate their actions towards others.

Review last week's lesson by going over any concerns or questions and summarize last week's objectives. Choose one participant to give a brief summary from last week. Review the homework assignment for this week. If using the optional point system, award points for homework completion and add to the group's total points. Review and post group rules.

Activity 4.1: Friendship Qualities

Overview: Girls will examine their friendship groups by evaluating what they value in a friendship. Girls will learn what a healthy friendship looks like, while being able to identify what kind of friend they are to others.

Objectives:
■ Girls will evaluate their friendship groups.
■ Girls will evaluate what they value in a friendship.
■ The girls will determine what makes a healthy friendship.
■ Girls will be able to identify what kind of friend they are.

Procedures:
■ Using an overhead, dry erase board, or the reproducible Activity 4.1 worksheet in Appendix A have the girls brainstorm their ideas about friendships.
■ Have the girls list various qualities and characteristics of friendship groups that can be both positive/healthy and negative/unhealthy on their worksheets.
■ Use the following discussion questions to help the girls brainstorm ideas.

Discussion Questions:
1. What do friendship groups look like (i.e. how many people are in a group)?
2. What do friendship groups do together?
   a. What are positive things (i.e. go to the movies, play sports, etc.)?
   b. What are negative things (i.e. gossip about others, exclude others, etc.)?

Activity 4.2: Friendship Qualities: Healthy vs. Unhealthy Friends

Overview: Girls will be able to brainstorm ideas about healthy and unhealthy characteristics of friendship groups. Girls will identify if they are in a healthy or unhealthy relationship with their friends.

Objectives:
- Girls will brainstorm ideas about healthy relationships.
- Girls will identify the characteristics or behaviors that can make friendships unhealthy.
- Girls will identify if they are in a healthy relationships with their friends.

Procedures:
- Copy Activity 4.2 found in Appendix A and hand out this worksheet to each girl.
- Have them complete this worksheet by listing the ideas they brainstormed about friendships from Activity 4.1 in the appropriate column.

Activity 4.3: Treating Others with Respect and Kindness

Overview: Girls will learn that healthy friendships include respecting and being kind to others even when it is difficult. Girls will learn how to develop and maintain healthy relationships with others.

Objectives:
- Girls will learn healthy friendship skills.
  - Respecting the rights of others
  - Being kind to others even when it is difficult to do so
- Girls will understand how negative actions or behaviors can lead to negative responses from others.
- Girls understand how positive actions or behaviors can lead to positive responses from others.
- Girls will use problem solving strategies to reframe negative actions into more positive actions.

Procedures:
- Reproduce Activity 4.3 found in Appendix A and hand out a copy of this worksheet to each of the girls.
- Read the situations and discuss whether the behavior was positive/acceptable or negative/unacceptable. Then, read how others responded to the behavior.
- Answer the following questions:
  - Did the behavior work? Did the girl get what she wanted by acting the way she did? How did her friends respond to her behavior?
  - How could she have shown her feelings in a more appropriate way? How would her friends have reacted to her if she acted in this way?

Activity 4.4: How People Respond to Me

Overview: Girls will evaluate and monitor how they treat others. Girls will be able to identify if they act in a healthy or unhealthy way towards others, while identifying if their behaviors help them to make friends.

Objectives:
- Girls will learn to respect the rights of others.
- Girls will identify if they act in a kind way towards others.
- Girls will evaluate their behavior or actions towards others.
- Girls will begin to monitor how they treat others.
- Girls will make the connection that negative treatment towards others can influence a negative response from others.

Procedures:
- Reproduce Activity 4.4 found in Appendix A and hand out a copy of this worksheet to each of the girls.
- Have the girls complete this activity by identifying a specific behavior or action given a certain situation. Write this behavior in the space provided on the worksheet.
- Next, have the girls answer the following questions by writing their answers in the appropriate space on the worksheet:
  - Did your behavior work for you? Did you get what you wanted by acting how you did? How did your friends respond to you?
- If the behavior they identified was unhealthy or negative, have them reframe the behavior. Write the reframed behavior in the appropriate space on the worksheet.
  - How differently would others respond to you if you had acted in a more positive way?

Activity 4.5: Measuring Up as a Friend

Overview: Girls will be able to identify the qualities and characteristics of a healthy friendship. Girls will be able to identify if their behavior helps them to develop and maintain friendships with others.

Objectives:
- Girls will identify the qualities and characteristics of healthy friendships.
- Girls will evaluate their behavior and decide if it contributes to developing and maintaining healthy friendships with others.
- Girls will learn to continually evaluate and monitor their behaviors and actions towards others.

Procedures:
- Have the girls evaluate how they measure up as a friend by looking back at the list they created for Activity 4.2. Have the girls go through each of the items they listed in both columns and decide if they do or do not do the things listed.
- Ask the girls to evaluate if they act in a healthy or unhealthy way by writing a yes or no next to each of the things listed in their columns.
- After the girls have gone through their list, have them rate what kind of friend they are overall (i.e. 1 = I need to work on my friendship skills, 5 = I have some work to do but I'm doing well with some things, 10 = I'm doing great as a friend).
- Use the following discussion questions to summarize the activities for this lesson.

Discussion Questions:
1. What qualities do healthy friendships or relationships have?
2. Are my relationships with others positive?
3. Which column do most of my friendship characteristics fall into?

4. Would I consider myself to be an acceptable or unacceptable friend?
5. What do I need to work on in order to be a better friend to others?
6. Do I do kind things for others?
7. Do I talk my problems out when I am angry with someone?

Activity 4.6: Relational Aggression Book Study

Overview: The girls will learn to empathize with others who have faced similar situations involving relational aggression through a book study.

Objectives:
■ Girls will understand what relational aggression or female bullying is.
■ Girls will learn to empathize with girls who are victims of relational aggression.
■ Girls will learn to take the perspective of others.
■ Girls will understand that relational aggression hurts both the aggressors and victims.

Procedures:
■ Read a passage from a book depicting relational aggression. See Appendix E for a list of sample books and passage selections.
■ Complete the following discussion questions by having the girls write their answers to the discussion questions on the reproducible Activity 4.6: Relational Aggression Book Study worksheet found in Appendix A.

Discussion Questions:
1. What was the mean behavior or relationally aggressive act observed?
2. Who was the victim in this passage? Who was the aggressor?
3. What did the victim do in this passage (i.e. were any strategies observed)?
4. What did the aggressor do in this passage?
5. Who was hurt in this passage? How were they hurt?
6. Describe any positive strategies that were used in this passage.

Activity 4.7: Question Cards — Healthy Friendships

Overview: Girls will demonstrate what they learned about healthy relationships and friendships. Girls will identify the qualities that make friendships healthy.

Objectives:
■ Girls will be able to identify what it means to have a healthy relationship or friendship.
■ Girls will be able to identify the qualities that make friendships healthy.

Procedures:
■ Hand out an index card to each group member, and have them write down one question they want clarified about relationships or friendships from this week's session. Or, have the girls write one thing they learned about friendships from this week's session.
■ Collect these cards as the girls leave.
■ Review these cards and discuss them prior to beginning session five's objectives.

Discussion Questions: (for discussion at the beginning of next week's session)
1. Were there any questions about friendships that need clarification?
2. Review a few key points or statements that were listed about friendships.

Activity 4.8: **Homework — Reframing My Actions**

Overview: The girls will generalize the information learned from the group session by completing homework for next week's session.

Objectives:
- Girls will write about a time when they acted in a negative way towards others.
- Girls will identify their thoughts, feelings, and actions.
- Girls will evaluate how their actions influenced how others responded to them.
- Girls will be able to reframe their behavior in a more positive way.

Procedures:
- Reproduce Activity 4.8: Homework in Appendix A for this activity.
- Hand out a copy of this worksheet to each girl, and have them complete this worksheet for next week's group session.
- Explain that these questions will be discussed next week.
- If using the point option, explain that girls can earn points for bringing back their completed homework next week.

Discussion Questions: (for discussion at the beginning of next week's session)
1. What was the situation?
2. What were you thinking in this situation?
3. How did you feel in this situation?
4. How did you act? What did you do?
5. How did others respond to you when you acted this way?
6. How could you have acted in a more appropriate or positive way?
7. How do you think others would have responded to you if you acted in a more positive way towards them?

Leader Notes for Group Session Four

Date: _____

Time: _____

Girls Present:

_____

_____

Girls Absent:

_____

_____

Summary of Session Four:

_____

_____

_____

What went well:

_____

_____

_____

What did not go well and may need improvement:

_____

_____

_____

Important notes:

_____

_____

_____

_____

S E S S I O N   F I V E :   (P A R T   1)

Healthy Social and Emotional Behaviors: Relational Aggression and Feelings

Purpose and Group Objectives
- Girls will define feelings and emotions.
- Girls will show their emotions in appropriate ways.
- Girls will recognize how their thoughts and feelings influence their actions.
- Girls will learn how their thoughts, feelings, and actions contribute to relational aggression.

Review last week's lesson by going over any concerns or questions and summarize last week's objectives. Choose one participant to give a brief summary from last week. Review the homework assignment for this week. If using the optional point system, award points for homework completion and add to the group's total points. Review and post group rules.

Activity 5.1: Feelings and Emotions

Overview: Girls will be able to define and identify various feelings or emotions. Girls will be able to identify how they are feeling given a certain situation, while understanding the purpose of emotions.

Objectives:
- Girls will be able to define what emotions or feelings are.
- Girls will identify various emotions.
- The girls will be able to identify how they are feeling given a specific situation.
- Girls will understand the purpose of emotions.
- Girls will understand the difference between thoughts and feelings.

Procedures:
- Refer to Activity 5.1 in Appendix A and make a copy of this worksheet for each girl.
- Lead the girls in a discussion about emotions or feelings. Use the discussion questions below as a guide.
- Following discussion, have girls complete Activity 5.1 by writing the two ways to identify emotions, the two purposes of emotions, and examples of emotions in the space provided on the worksheet.

Discussion Questions:
1. What are feelings and emotions?
2. Why do we have feelings and emotions?
3. How can we recognize our feelings?
4. How do our thoughts influence our feelings?
5. How do our bodies or physical symptoms influence our feelings?
6. How can our emotions affect whether or not relational aggression happens?

Discussion Points:
- Emotions or feelings tell us about something and allows us to change what is happening or what we are doing.
- We can recognize our feelings mentally (i.e. our thinking can influence how we are feeling) and physically (i.e. our physical symptoms can influence how we feel).
- Our emotions play a role in relational aggression. Relational aggression can happen when girls feel jealous of others, feel afraid of being rejected, or feel poorly or too highly about themselves (i.e. have very low or extremely high self-esteem).

Activity 5.2: Normal Feelings

Overview: Girls will understand that all feelings are okay and normal to have. Girls will learn to act in more appropriate ways when they feel angry/mad, upset, and sad.

Objectives:
- Girls will understand that all feelings are okay and normal to have.
- Girls will identify acceptable and unacceptable ways to show how they feel.
- The girls will learn that unacceptable ways of showing their feelings can lead to being relationally aggressive with others.
- Girls will be able to differentiate between positive and negative ways to deal with aggression and anger.

Procedures:
- Complete the Activity 5.2: Normal Feelings worksheet found in Appendix A.
- Lead the girls in a discussion about acceptable and unacceptable feelings. Use the discussion questions below as a guide.
- After the discussion, have the girls complete this worksheet by writing their answers on the blanks provided.
- Separate girls into small groups, and have them list both positive and negative ways to show how someone can act when they feel angry with a friend.

Discussion Questions:
1. Are all emotions or feelings acceptable or okay to have?
2. Is it normal to feel angry/mad, upset, or sad?
3. Is it okay to spread a rumor, exclude, or isolate someone if they did this to you first?
4. How do we show others how we feel in negative ways?
5. How do we show others how we feel in a positive ways?

Discussion Points:
- It is normal and acceptable to have all emotions (including anger). Some emotions can be pleasant (positive) or unpleasant (negative). Conflict in friendship groups and among friends is going to happen. Note: you may need to explain that having certain emotions that are extreme and chronic is not normal. Girls who feel that their emotions are constant and severe need to seek out adult help.
- All behaviors or actions in response to how we feel are not acceptable. Help girls to understand that getting revenge on others is not acceptable behavior even if someone was mean to them first. Being a bully back to someone will not make the situation better, often times it will only make the situation worse.

Activity 5.3: **Thinking, Feeling and Relational Aggression**

Overview: Girls will understand how their thoughts and emotions influence how they act towards others. Girls will learn that they are in control over their thoughts, feelings, and behaviors. Girls will understand how their thoughts, emotions, and behaviors contribute to relational aggression.

Objectives:

- Girls will identify that their thoughts and feelings influence their actions.
- Girls will recognize how their thoughts and feelings influence what they do.
- The girls will learn that they are in control of their thoughts, feelings, and actions.
- Girls will understand how their thoughts, feelings, and actions contribute to relational aggression.
- Girls will learn how to turn negative thoughts, feelings, and actions into something more positive.

Procedures:

- Refer to Activity 5.3 found in Appendix A. There are two pages for this activity. The first page can be reproduced and handed out, or it can be copied onto an overhead. Reproduce and hand out the second page to all girls.
- Read each of the listed scenarios on the first page and decide how each girl's thinking influenced how she felt and how this feeling influenced how she acted. Use the discussion questions below to guide the discussion.
- Have the girls provide examples of thoughts, emotions, and behaviors. Go over these examples as a whole group using the discussion questions as a guide.
- Independently, have the girls work through their own example on the second page worksheet by writing in their thoughts, emotions, and actions given a specific situation.

Discussion Questions:

1. What was the thought that this girl had? Was the thought negative or positive?
2. How did she feel because of what she thought? Was the feeling negative or positive?
3. What did she do because of how she felt? Was the action negative or positive?

Activity 5.4: **Role Play Scenarios — Understanding Feelings**

Overview: Girls will apply the skills they learned throughout this session through role playing. The girls will learn to understand how their thinking affects how they feel and what they do. Girls will learn to control their thoughts, feelings, and actions in a positive way.

Objectives:

- Girls will use problem solving skills.
- The girls will identify their feelings given a specific scenario of relational aggression.
- Girls will identify their thoughts given a specific scenario of relational aggression.
- Girls will demonstrate positive or appropriate ways to show how they would handle a situation involving relational aggression.

Procedures:

- Separate the girls into small groups and hand out a role play scenario to each group. The scenarios are included in Appendix A. It is recommended that you cut and paste each scenario on card stock or an index card prior to handing them out.

- Have each group read their scenario card and complete the questions on their worksheets for Activity 5.4 in Appendix A.
- After each group has answered the questions, have each group report out to the whole group by summarizing their scenarios while providing the answers to the questions on their worksheet. The questions are also listed below.

Discussion Questions:
1. What would you think in this situation?
2. How would you feel in this situation? What emotions would you have?
3. What would you do if this happened to you?
4. List two positive or appropriate ways to show how you feel without hurting others.

Activity 5.5: Relational Aggression Book Study

Overview: The girls will learn to empathize with others who have faced similar situations involving relational aggression through a book study.

Objectives:
- Girls will understand what relational aggression or female bullying is.
- Girls will learn to empathize with girls who are victims of relational aggression.
- Girls will learn to take the perspective of others.
- Girls will understand that relational aggression hurts both the aggressors and victims.

Procedures:
- Read a passage from a book depicting relational aggression. See Appendix E for a list of sample books and passage selections.
- Complete the following discussion questions by having the girls write their answers to the discussion questions on the reproducible Activity 5.5: Relational Aggression Book Study worksheet found in Appendix A.

Discussion Questions:
1. What was the mean behavior or relationally aggressive act observed?
2. Who was the victim in this passage? Who was the aggressor?
3. What did the victim do in this passage (i.e. were any strategies observed)?
4. What did the aggressor do in this passage?
5. Who was hurt in this passage? How were they hurt?
6. Describe any positive strategies that were used in this passage.

Activity 5.6: What I Know Now

Overview: Girls will reflect upon what they have learned so far from this group. Girls will identify what new facts or knowledge they have learned about relational aggression. Girls will identify if their beliefs about relational aggression have changed in some way.

Objectives:
- Girls will evaluate if their knowledge of relational aggression has increased since session one.
- The girls will evaluate if their beliefs about relational aggression have changed since session one.

Procedures:
- Have the girls refer back to Activity 1.4 to complete this activity.
- Have the girls review what they wrote on the top part of their worksheet. What did they know about relational aggression at the beginning of session one? What did they want to learn about relational aggression?
- Have the girls complete the bottom part of this worksheet by writing their answers by the lines provided. What have the girls learned about relational aggression? Are their beliefs about relational aggression the same or have they changed since session one?

Discussion Questions:
1. What did the girls know about relational aggression at the beginning of session one?
2. Has their knowledge about relational aggression increased from session one?
3. What did the girls want to learn about relational aggression?
4. Are there still things that they want to learn about relational aggression?
5. What did girls believe about relational aggression from session one?
6. Have their beliefs about relational aggression changed in some way?

Activity 5.7: Question Cards — Feelings and Emotions

Overview: Girls will demonstrate what they have learned about feelings and emotions. Girls will demonstrate how their thoughts, feelings, and actions relate to relational aggression.

Objectives:
- Girls will demonstrate what they have learned about feelings and emotions.
- Girls will identify how their thinking, feeling, and behaviors can prevent relational aggression.

Procedures:
- Hand out an index card to each group member, and have them write down one question they want clarified about feelings and emotions from this week's session. Or, have the girls write one thing they learned about feelings and relational aggression.
- Collect these cards as the girls leave.
- Review these cards and discuss them prior to beginning session six's objectives.

Discussion Questions: (for discussion at the beginning of next week's session)
1. Were there any questions about feelings and emotions that need clarification?
2. Review a few key points or statements about feelings and relational aggression.

Activity 5.8: Homework — Thoughts, Feelings, Actions

Overview: The girls will generalize the information learned from the group session by completing homework for next week's session.

Objectives:
- Girls will describe the emotion they had in a situation involving relational aggression.
- Girls will be able to identify the thoughts they had in this situation.
- Girls will be able to identify the feelings they had in this situation.
- Girls will demonstrate that they solved this situation in a positive way.

Procedures:
- Reproduce Activity 5.8: Homework in Appendix A for this activity.
- Hand out a copy of this worksheet to each girl, and have them complete this worksheet for next week's group session.
- Explain that these questions will be discussed next week.
- If using the point option, explain that girls can earn points for bringing back their completed homework next week.

Discussion Questions: (for discussion at the beginning of next week's session)
1. What was the situation?
2. What did you think about the situation?
3. How did you feel about the situation? What emotion did you have?
4. What did you do in the situation as a result of what you thought and felt?

Leader Notes for Group Session Five

Date: _____

Time: _____

Girls Present:

_____

_____

Girls Absent:

_____

_____

Summary of Session Five:

_____

_____

_____

What went well:

_____

_____

_____

What did not go well and may need improvement:

_____

_____

_____

Important notes:

_____

_____

_____

_____

Healthy Social and Emotional Behaviors: Relational Aggression and Empathy

Purpose and Group Objectives

- Girls will define empathy.
- Girls will show empathy for others.
- Girls will understand what it means to take the perspective of others.
- Girls will appreciate the differences in others.

Review last week's lesson by going over any concerns or questions and summarize last week's objectives. Choose one participant to give a brief summary from last week. Review the homework assignment for this week. If using the optional point system, award points for homework completion and add to the group's total points. Review and post group rules.

Activity 6.1: Empathy

Overview: Girls will understand what it means to have empathy for someone else. Girls will be able to show empathy towards others.

Objectives:
- Girls will be able to define and understand empathy.
- The girls will be able to list examples of empathy.
- Girls will show empathy towards others.

Procedures:
- Copy and hand out Activity 6.1: Empathy in Appendix A.
- Lead the girls in a discussion about empathy using the discussion questions below.
- Have the girls complete this worksheet by listing other examples of empathy in the space provided.
- Then have the girls complete the bottom portion of this worksheet by reading each situation and deciding how they could show empathy. Answers can be written in the space provided on this worksheet.

Discussion Questions:
1. What does empathy mean?
2. What are examples of empathy?
3. How can showing empathy for others help prevent relational aggression?

Discussion Points:
- Empathy means having compassion for someone else and understanding how they feel. Empathy is being able to understand how another person feels emotionally.

- Examples of empathy include: asking someone to sit with you at lunch when they have no place to sit, writing a friendly note to cheer someone up, having compassion for someone who is being excluded from a group by including them, befriending someone who is new to school.
- Being empathetic towards others allows one to stop and think about the other person's situation before acting in a way that will hurt them (i.e. if we have been unable to afford new clothes at one time, we will be more empathetic for someone else who cannot afford to buy trendy clothes and will be less likely to say hurtful things about their choice of clothing).

Activity 6.2: Taking the Perspective of Others

Overview: Girls will learn what it means to take the perspective of others. Girls will learn that other people think and feel differently in the same situation. The girls will understand that different opinions can sometimes lead to positive changes.

Objectives:
- Girls will understand what it means to take the perspective of others.
- Girls will learn that other people think and feel differently in the same situation.
- Girls will begin to appreciate the different opinions and thoughts of others.
- Girls will see that different opinions can lead to positive changes.

Procedures:
- Copy and hand out Activity 6.2: Taking the Perspective of Others worksheet in Appendix A.
- First lead the girls in a discussion about perspective taking. The discussion questions and points below can be used as a guide.
- In the space provided on the worksheet, have the girls write down an influential person from history that changed the world in an important way because of the point of view or perspective that they had. List who the person was, what the point of view was, and the impact it had on the world.
- Next, have the girls think of a time when they have had a different opinion or perspective from someone else and the impact it had. Or, have the girls choose someone from their life to write about. List who the person was, what the point of view was, and the impact it had on this worksheet.

Discussion Questions:
1. What does it mean to take the perspective of others?
2. Can it be bad to have an opinion different from someone else?
3. Is all conflict or disagreement with others bad?

Discussion Points:
- Taking the perspective of others means looking at things from another individual's point of view, and understanding that other people have opinions and feelings that are different given the same situation.
- Having an opinion different from others is not a bad thing. Everyone has different opinions and ideas that can contribute in some way.
- Different opinions can often lead to positive changes, because they can make us compromise and work to change or improve the way things are currently.

Activity 6.3: **Role Play — Empathy and the Perspective of Others Scenarios**

Overview: Girls will learn how to evaluate the same situation in more than one way. Girls will apply the empathy and understanding skills they have learned by identifying how others feel given different situations.

Objectives:

- Girls will be able to identify how others feel given a scenario of relational aggression.
- Girls will show empathy for someone else.
- Girls will understand what it means to take the perspective of others.

Procedures:

- Separate the girls into small groups for this activity.
- Using the scenarios in Appendix A, hand out a different scenario card to each group. You may want to copy and paste each scenario on card stock or an index card.
- Have the girls read each scenario and answer the discussion questions using the Activity 6.3 worksheet located in Appendix A.
- After each group has answered the questions, have them report out to the whole group by summarizing their scenario and answers to the questions.

Discussion Questions:

1. What is the emotion that each person in this situation felt?
2. Are there any clues that tell you how each person might feel?
3. Did everyone in the group think that each person in the situation felt the same? Why or why not?
4. Why is it important to see things from the perspective of others?
5. How could you show empathy in each of these scenarios?

Activity 6.4: **Relational Aggression Book Study**

Overview: The girls will learn to empathize with others who have faced similar situations involving relational aggression through a book study.

Objectives:

- Girls will understand what relational aggression or female bullying is.
- Girls will learn to empathize with girls who are victims of relational aggression.
- Girls will learn to take the perspective of others.
- Girls will understand that relational aggression hurts both the aggressors and victims.

Procedures:

- Read a passage from a book depicting relational aggression. See Appendix E for a list of sample books and passage selections.
- Complete the following discussion questions by having the girls write their answers to the discussion questions on the reproducible Activity 6.4: Relational Aggression Book Study worksheet found in Appendix A.

Discussion Questions:

1. What was the mean behavior or relationally aggressive act observed?
2. Who was the victim in this passage? Who was the aggressor?
3. What did the victim do in this passage (i.e. were any strategies observed)?
4. What did the aggressor do in this passage?
5. Who was hurt in this passage? How were they hurt?
6. Describe any positive strategies that were used in this passage.

Activity 6.5: Question Cards — Empathy

Overview: Girls will demonstrate what they know about empathy and perspective taking. Girls will understand how relational aggression is related to empathy and perspective taking.

Objectives:

- Girls will gain a better understanding of empathy and perspective taking.
- Girls will identify how empathy and perspective taking relate to relational aggression.

Procedures:

- Hand out an index card to each group member, and have them write down one question they want clarified about empathy and/or perspective taking from this week's session. Or, have the girls write one thing they learned about empathy and/or perspective taking.
- Collect these cards as the girls leave.
- Review these cards and discuss them prior to beginning session seven's objectives.

Discussion Questions: (for discussion at the beginning of next week's session)

1. Were there any questions about empathy and/or perspective taking that need clarification?
2. Review a few key points or statements that were listed about empathy and perspective taking.

Activity 6.6: Homework — Perspective Change

Overview: The girls will review the information learned from the group session by completing homework for next week's session.

Objectives:

- Girls will describe a time that their perspective changed in some way.
- Girls will be able to identify the thoughts they had in this situation.
- Girls will be able to identify the feelings they had in this situation.

Procedures:

- Reproduce Activity 6.6: Homework in Appendix A for this activity.
- Hand out a copy of this worksheet to each girl, and have them complete this worksheet for next week's group session.
- Explain that these questions will be discussed next week.
- If using the point option, explain that girls can earn points for bringing back their completed homework next week.

Discussion Questions: (for discussion at the beginning of next week's session)
1. What was the situation?
2. How did your perspective about something change?
3. What did you think about the situation?
4. How did you feel about the situation?

Leader Notes for Group Session Six

Date: _____

Time: _____

Girls Present:

_____

_____

Girls Absent:

_____

_____

Summary of Session Six:

_____

_____

_____

What went well:

_____

_____

_____

What did not go well and may need improvement:

_____

_____

_____

Important notes:

_____

_____

_____

Building Self-Confidence

Purpose and Group Objectives
- Girls will understand that they have many abilities that make them unique.
- Girls will identify what self-esteem is.
- Girls will identify what abilities they have.
- Girls will develop a positive self-esteem by being kind to others.

Review last week's lesson by going over any concerns or questions and summarize last week's objectives. Choose one participant to give a brief summary from last week. Review the homework assignment for this week. If using the optional point system, award points for homework completion and add to the group's total points. Review and post group rules.

Activity 7.1: Unique Me

Overview: Girls will understand that they have many unique abilities that contribute to who they are. Girls will learn to appreciate the qualities in themselves, while appreciating the qualities within others.

Objectives:
- Girls will understand that they have many abilities that make them unique.
- Girls will identify the many roles they play.
- Girls will identify the various characteristics they have.
- Girls will identify how they feel about themselves.

Procedures:
- Copy and hand out Activity 7.1: Unique Me in Appendix A.
- Have the girls complete this activity by listing what makes them unique. Have the girls list characteristics, abilities, strengths, and the roles that they play that make them unique by the lines on this worksheet.
- Facilitate a discussion using the discussion questions below after each girl has completed their worksheet.

Discussion Questions:
1. Have the girls review their answers.
   - What characteristics (i.e. funny, smart) did each girl list? Did everyone list the same characteristics?
   - What abilities did each girl list (i.e. good at sports, good at math)? Did everyone list that they were good at the same things?
   - What roles did each girl list (i.e. sister, student)? Did everyone list the same roles?

2. What defines you or makes you unique from someone else?

Discussion Point:
- Explain to the girls that there are many unique characteristics, abilities, roles, and strengths that make each of us who we are. We all have been given certain talents and abilities that make us unique and different from others.

Activity 7.2: **My Self-Esteem and Self-Talk**

Overview: Girls will define what it means to have a positive self-esteem and be self-confident. Girls will identify the factors that contribute to having a positive self-esteem.

Objectives:
- Girls will define what it means to have self-esteem.
- Girls will identify their own self-esteem.
- Girls will define what it means to be self-confident.
- Girls will understand that their thoughts and feelings about themselves contribute to their self-esteem and self-confidence.
- Girls will understand how self-esteem and self-confidence relates to relational aggression.

Procedures:
- Reproduce Activity 7.2: My Self-Esteem and Self-Talk in Appendix A. Hand out a copy of this worksheet to each of the girls.
- Using the discussion questions and points below, have the girls answer what it means to have self-esteem and self-confidence by writing their answers on the lines provided in this worksheet.
- Have the girls evaluate their self-esteem by examining what their self-talk is like. Have them fill in the chart on their worksheet by listing the thoughts and feelings they have about themselves, the goals they have, and the influences that other people have on them. Note: you may want to refer to session nine for more detailed information about goals and goal setting for this activity.
- Have the girls complete this activity by answering the remaining two questions on the worksheet page. Discuss the last question using the discussion points below.

Discussion Questions:
1. What is self-esteem?
2. What does being self-confident mean?
3. Is it okay to show confidence in your abilities? Is it okay to feel good about yourself?
4. Is it possible to feel too highly, or too good, about yourself?

Discussion Points:
- Self-esteem is how we feel about ourselves. If we view ourselves in a positive way, we are more likely to feel good about ourselves and have a positive self-esteem. If we see ourselves in a negative way, we are more likely to feel bad about ourselves.
- Self-confidence means being sure and confident in yourself and your abilities. Girls who are self-confident and have a positive self-esteem are less likely to bully others. Girls who have positive self-esteems do not need to hurt others in order to get what they want or need to make themselves feel better or above others.
- Self-esteem and self-confidence are influenced by the way we think and feel about ourselves. If we think and feel negative thoughts about ourselves, we are likely to have a lower sense of self-esteem. If we let others define us and how we think and feel about ourselves, we are likely to perceive that we have less control over our self perceptions. We can create a positive self-esteem by thinking and feeling positively, learning to set personal goals for ourselves, and accepting constructive criticism in order to improve the things that we need to work on individually.
- It is okay and acceptable to be self-confident in your abilities and feel good about yourself. It is possible to feel too highly about yourself by not being able to accept constructive criticism from others and feeling that it is okay to bully others because they are different from you.

Activity 7.3: **My Self-View: Who I Want to Be**

Overview: Girls will determine how they want to be perceived by others, as well as by themselves. Girls will reflect on whether or not their actions match their ideas of how they want to be viewed.

Objectives:

- Girls will summarize what makes them unique (i.e. values, strengths, weaknesses).
- Girls will determine what kind of reputation they want to have.
- Girls will examine if their actions match how they want to be viewed by others.

Procedures:

- Copy and hand out Activity 7.3: My Self-View: Who I Want to Be worksheet found in Appendix A. Have the girls use their ideas from Activities 7.1 and 7.2 to complete this activity.
- Have the girls summarize the previous activities from this session by writing the things that make them unique in the space provided on the worksheet. Then, have them answer the questions on this handout.
- *(Optional) Extension Activity:* Provide girls with magazines, paper, markers, colored paper, and writing tools in order for them to make representations of themselves.
  - Example representations may include: collages using pictures from magazines that would include activities they are involved in or characteristics that would describe them, drawings of themselves, a poem that describes their talents, a song written about their aspirations and characteristics, a book about the many roles they play
- *(Optional) Extension Activity:* Have the girls share their representations.
  - Have each girl share the representation they created by illustrating what makes each of them unique from others as well as similar to others. The discussion questions below can be used as follow up questions.
  - Hand out index cards to each of the girls. Each girl should receive enough index cards in order to write a positive comment for each girl's representation to the group. Explain that these cards will be collected and given to the appropriate recipient.
  - Collect all of the cards and hand them out to the appropriate recipient after all the representations have been shared. Note: you may want to read these cards to ensure that all comments are positive prior to handing the cards out to each of the girls.

Discussion Questions:

1. Did you share similarities with anyone else in the group? What were the similarities?
2. How was your representation different from others in the group?
3. Did you learn something new about someone else in the group?
4. What was something positive that someone added to this group?

Activity 7.4 **Kindness Matters**

Overview: Girls will develop positive self-esteem skills by being kind to others. Girls will feel good about themselves by being able to compliment others. Girls will evaluate how acts of kindness can influence one's thoughts, feelings, and behaviors. Girls will evaluate how acts of kindness can influence the behaviors of others.

Objectives:

- Girls will develop positive self-esteem skills by being kind to others.
- Girls will learn how to compliment others.

- Girls will evaluate how kindness can influence how one thinks, feels, and acts.
- Girls will evaluate how kindness can influence how others respond to them.

Procedures:
- Hand out an index card to each of the girls, and have the girls list one way that they could show kindness towards someone else.
  - Example ideas might include: asking a girl to sit with your group at the lunch table, including an excluded girl, helping someone in a specific way, giving someone a compliment
- Collect the cards and randomly distribute a card to each of the girls. Explain that they will need to complete what is written on their card for homework next week. Hand out the homework sheet in Appendix A.
- *Extension Activity:* Separate the girls into groups of two. Have them take turns and practice acting out what is written on their card prior to having to do this for homework.

Activity 7.5: Relational Aggression Book Study

Overview: The girls will learn to empathize with others who have faced similar situations involving relational aggression through a book study.

Objectives:
- Girls will understand what relational aggression or female bullying is.
- Girls will learn to empathize with girls who are victims of relational aggression.
- Girls will learn to take the perspective of others.
- Girls will understand that relational aggression hurts both the aggressors and victims.

Procedures:
- Read a passage from a book depicting relational aggression. See Appendix E for a list of sample books and passage selections.
- Complete the following discussion questions by having the girls write their answers to the discussion questions on the reproducible Activity 7.5: Relational Aggression Book Study worksheet found in Appendix A.

Discussion Questions:
1. What was the mean behavior or relationally aggressive act observed?
2. Who was the victim in this passage? Who was the aggressor?
3. What did the victim do in this passage (i.e. were any strategies observed)?
4. What did the aggressor do in this passage?
5. Who was hurt in this passage? How were they hurt?
6. Describe any positive strategies that were used in this passage.

Activity 7.6: Question Cards — Self-Esteem

Overview: Girls will demonstrate what they have learned about self-esteem and self-confidence.

Objectives:
- Girls will demonstrate their knowledge of self-esteem and self-confidence.
- Girls will identify what they still want to know about self-esteem and self-confidence.

Procedures:

- Hand out an index card to each group member, and have them write down one thing they learned about self-esteem and/or self-confidence from today's session. Or, have them write down one question they have about self-esteem and/or self-confidence from today's session.
- Collect these cards as the girls leave.
- Review these cards and discuss them prior to beginning session eight's objectives.

Discussion Questions: (for discussion at the beginning of next week's session)

1. Were there any questions about self-esteem and/or self-confidence that need clarification?
2. Review a few key points or statements that were listed about self-esteem and/or self-confidence.

Activity 7.7: Homework — Influences of kindness

Overview: The girls will generalize the information learned from the group session by completing homework for next week's session.

Objectives:

- Girls will evaluate how kindness influenced how one thought, felt, and acted.
- Girls will evaluate how kindness influenced how others responded to them.
- Girls will demonstrate more prosocial behaviors.

Procedures:

- Reproduce Activity 7.7: Homework in Appendix A for this activity.
- Hand out a copy of this worksheet to each girl, and have them complete this worksheet for next week's group session.
- Explain that these questions will be discussed next week.
- If using the point option, explain that girls can earn points for bringing back their completed homework next week.

Discussion Questions: (for discussion at the beginning of next week's session)

1. What was the act of kindness on your index card?
2. What was the situation? When did you act out what was written on your card?
3. What did you think about the situation?
3. How did you feel about the situation?
4. How did the other person respond to you after you were nice to them?

Leader Notes for Group Session Seven

Date: _____

Time: _____

Girls Present:

_____

_____

Girls Absent:

_____

_____

Summary of Session Seven:

_____

_____

_____

What went well:

_____

_____

_____

What did not go well and may need improvement:

_____

_____

_____

Important notes:

_____

_____

_____

_____

SESSION EIGHT:

Challenging Negative Beliefs

Purpose and Group Objectives
- Girls will take responsibility for the choices they make.
- Girls will understand that all choices have consequences.
- Girls will learn to use problem solving.
- Girls will learn how their choices can influence certain outcomes.

Review last week's lesson by going over any concerns or questions and summarize last week's objectives. Choose one participant to give a brief summary from last week. Review the homework assignment for this week. If using the optional point system, award points for homework completion and add to the group's total points. Review and post group rules.

Activity 8.1: Problem Solving and My Belief System

Overview: Girls will learn and use problem solving strategies when relational aggression occurs. Girls will learn that they are responsible for the choices they make and the beliefs they have about a situation.

Objectives:
- Girls will learn and use problem solving strategies.
- Girls will stop and think about a situation before reacting hastily.
- Girls will take responsibility for the choices they make.
- The girls will understand that every choice has a consequence.
- Girls will understand how their choices can influence negative and positive outcomes.

Procedures:
- Use the Activity 8.1: Problem Solving and My Belief System Chart (Worksheet #2) included in Appendix A to teach the girls about problem solving. There are two worksheets for this activity.
  - The acronym S.T.O.P. can help the girls remember the steps involved in problem solving.

    S = *Situation*:   What is the situation or problem?

    T = *Thoughts*:   What am I thinking in this situation?

    O = *Options*:   What can I choose to do? What would happen next?

    P = *Progress*:   Did my choice work? Do I need to do something else?

- As a whole group, discuss the problem solving steps by working through the example provided in Activity 8.1: Problem Solving and My Belief System Chart.
- Have the girls answer the four questions on the Problem Solving and My Belief System worksheet.

Activity 8.2: Problem Solving in Action

Overview: Girls will be able to apply specific problem solving strategies in a real life example related to relational aggression. Girls will take responsibility for their behavior by understanding that the choices they make have consequences.

Objectives:
- Girls will learn what problem solving is.
- Girls will learn how to effectively use a problem solving chart.
- Girls will learn that they are responsible for their actions and how they treat others.
- Girls will understand that all choices have negative or positive consequences.

Procedures:
- Hand out the Activity 8.2: Problem Solving in Action worksheet and the Activity 8.2: Problem Solving and My Belief System Chart from Appendix A.
- Have the girls think of a real life situation involving relational aggression. Have the girls use the blank problem solving chart to answer the four problem solving questions. The four questions are also listed on the Problem Solving in Action worksheet.
- After the girls have finished completing their charts, choose two or three examples to review. Use the discussion questions below to determine if the girls understand how to use the problem solving steps when relational aggression happens.

Discussion Questions:
1. Discuss the charts using the problem solving steps:
    - What was the situation or problem related to relational aggression?
    - What were your thoughts or beliefs about the situation?
    - How did you feel in this situation? What was the emotion or feeling?
    - What options did you think of in this situation? What did you decide to do?
    - What was the progress or outcome because of the choice you made? Did it/would it work or do you need to try another option?
2. Are there any questions about the problem solving steps?

Activity 8.3: Relational Aggression Book Study

Overview: The girls will learn to empathize with others who have faced similar situations involving relational aggression through a book study.

Objectives:
- Girls will understand what relational aggression or female bullying is.
- Girls will learn to empathize with girls who are victims of relational aggression.
- Girls will learn to take the perspective of others.
- Girls will understand that relational aggression hurts both the aggressors and victims.

Procedures:
- Read a passage from a book depicting relational aggression. See Appendix E for a list of sample books and passage selections.
- Complete the following discussion questions by having the girls write their answers to the discussion questions on the reproducible Activity 8.3: Relational Aggression Book Study worksheet found in Appendix A.

Discussion Questions:

1. What was the mean behavior or relationally aggressive act observed?
2. Who was the victim in this passage? Who was the aggressor?
3. What did the victim do in this passage (i.e. were any strategies observed)?
4. What did the aggressor do in this passage?
5. Who was hurt in this passage? How were they hurt?
6. Describe any positive strategies that were used in this passage.

Activity 8.4: Question Cards — Problem Solving

Overview: Girls will demonstrate what they know about problem solving. Girls will demonstrate how problem solving can be used when relational aggression occurs.

Objectives:

- Girls will demonstrate their knowledge of problem solving.
- Girls will identify what they would still like to know about problem solving and relational aggression.

Procedures:

- Hand out an index card to each group member, and have them write down one thing they learned about problem solving from today's session. Or, have the girls write one question they have about problem solving from today's session.
- Collect these cards as the girls leave.
- Review these cards and discuss them prior to beginning session nine's objectives.

Discussion Questions: (for discussion at the beginning of next week's session)

1. Were there any questions about problem solving that need clarification?
2. Review a few key points or statements that were listed about problem solving.

Activity 8.5: Homework — Group Project

Overview: The girls will demonstrate their knowledge of relational aggression or female bullying. Girls will demonstrate the strategies they learned for treating relational aggression. Girls will demonstrate how they used problem solving and cooperative strategies when working with others.

Objectives:

- Girls will demonstrate their knowledge of relational aggression.
- Girls will demonstrate strategies for treating relational aggression.
- Girls will show that they learned how to work cooperatively with others.
- Girls will demonstrate the problem solving skills that they have learned.

Procedures:

- Remind the girls that group projects about relational aggression are due next week.
- Explain that these projects must teach others what relational aggression is.
- Explain that these projects must teach others how to approach relational aggression.
- Girls will present these projects next week during the group session.
  - Example ideas may include: a play about relational aggression/female bullying, making a poster or collage about healthy relationships, designing an after school club for girls, creating a game about relational aggression, power point presentation, newsletter, brochure, crossword puzzle, role play activities, or a book about relational aggression

Leader Notes for Group Session Eight

Date: _____

Time: _____

Girls Present:

_____

_____

Girls Absent:

_____

_____

Summary of Session Eight:

_____

_____

_____

What went well:

_____

_____

_____

What did not go well and may need improvement:

_____

_____

_____

Important notes:

_____

_____

_____

_____

SESSION NINE:
Relational Aggression and the Future

Purpose and Group Objectives
- Girls will demonstrate an increase in their knowledge of relational aggression.
- Girls will demonstrate change in their belief systems about relational aggression.
- Girls will identify what a goal and goal setting is.
- Girls will show how they can prevent and stop relational aggression.

Review last week's lesson by going over any concerns or questions and summarize last week's objectives. Choose one participant to give a brief summary from last week. Review the homework assignment for this week. If using the optional point system, award points for homework completion and add to the group's total points. Present an award to the group if they reached their goal.

Activity 9.1: What I Know Now

Overview: Girls will reflect upon what they have learned from this group. Girls will identify what new facts or knowledge they have learned about relational aggression. Girls will identify if their beliefs about relational aggression have changed.

Objectives:
- Girls will evaluate if their knowledge of relational aggression has increased since sessions one and five.
- The girls will evaluate if their beliefs about relational aggression have changed since sessions one and five.

Procedures:
- Have the girls refer back to Activity 1.4 in order to complete this activity.
- Have the girls review what they wrote on the top part of their worksheet. Use the following questions to help the girls reflect on this activity.
  - What did they know about relational aggression at the beginning of session one? What did they want to learn about relational aggression?
- Have the girls review the bottom part of this worksheet. Use the following questions to help the girls reflect on this activity.
  - What did the girls know about relational aggression by session five? Are their beliefs about relational aggression the same or have they changed since session five?
- Have the girls write in any new information that they have learned about relational aggression since session five on their worksheets. Have the girls list any new beliefs that they now have about relational aggression on this worksheet.

Activity 9.2: Setting Goals

Overview: Girls will understand what goal setting is. Girls will be able to see the connection that goal setting has on one's thoughts, feelings, and behaviors. Girls will understand how setting goals can lead to healthy friendships and a positive self-esteem.

Objectives:
- Girls will be able to define what a goal is.
- Girls will be able to define what goal setting is.
- Girls will understand how setting goals can help them change their thoughts, feelings, and behaviors.
- Girls will understand how setting goals can help them define what is appropriate and inappropriate girl behavior.
- Girls will learn that goal setting can help cultivate a positive self-esteem.

Procedures:
- Copy and hand out Activity 9.2: Setting Goals found in Appendix A.
- Lead the girls in a discussion about goals and goal setting. The discussion questions and points below can be used to facilitate a discussion.
- Have the girls complete this activity by brainstorming possible goals that they would like to achieve. Have them list these goals on the space provided on their worksheets.
  - Sample goals might include: using assertiveness skills when angry, saying more positive things about oneself, being more empathetic towards others, appreciating the differences in others
- Have the girls complete the bottom part of this worksheet by going through the goal setting process. Have the girls pick one goal that they want to achieve and go through the goal setting steps, G.O.A.L.

Discussion Questions:
1. What is a goal?
2. What kind of goals are there?
3. What do you have to do in order to achieve your goals?
4. How does goal setting relate to my thoughts, feelings, and behaviors?
5. How can goal setting help me with my friendships?

Discussion Points:
- A goal is something that someone wants and is willing to work for. Goals can be short term (right now) or long term (future).
- Goals can be academic and/or behavioral. Academic goals might include things like getting good grades, turning in and completing homework, and making the honor roll. Behavioral goals might include things like using empathy more, being more assertive, and exercising more.
- One can use a goal setting process to achieve goals. First, identify the goals you want to achieve. Second, think about the options that will help you get your goal. Third, choose an option and act it out. Fourth, evaluate if you reached your goal. If you did not achieve it, ask yourself what you need to do differently.
- Setting goals allows one the opportunity to change thoughts, feelings, and behaviors. We can set a goal to change our thinking if we are constantly thinking negatively. We can set a goal to change our negative feelings. And we can set a goal if we want to change how we are acting.
- Goals allow us to define what acceptable and unacceptable behaviors within our friendship groups are.
  - Friendship goals might include: people will get along with each other, we will use assertiveness skills to talk out our problems when conflict happens, we will respect the rights of others by including everyone and refrain from intentionally acting in a way that could hurt others

Activity 9.3: Group Project

Overview: The girls will demonstrate their knowledge of relational aggression or female bullying. Girls will demonstrate the strategies they learned for treating relational aggression. Girls will demonstrate how they used problem solving and cooperative strategies when working with others.

Objectives:
- Girls will demonstrate their knowledge of relational aggression.
- Girls will demonstrate strategies for stopping relational aggression.
- Girls will show that they learned how to work cooperatively with others.
- Girls will demonstrate the problem solving skills that they have learned.

Procedures:
- Have the girls demonstrate their group projects.
- The discussion questions below can be used to facilitate the girl's knowledge of relational aggression following their presentation.
- *Extension Activity:* Have the girls present their projects to other classrooms where relational aggression is a problem.

Discussion Questions:
1. What is relational aggression or female bullying?
2. How did you demonstrate your knowledge of relational aggression?
3. How does this teach others about relational aggression?
4. What strategies can others use to stop relational aggression?
5. How did you and your partner work cooperatively with one another?
6. Was it easy to complete this project? Why or why not?

Activity 9.4: Relational Aggression Assessment Measure

Overview: Girls will demonstrate their knowledge about relational aggression following implementation of the relational aggression curriculum. Girls will indicate if their beliefs about relational aggression have changed in some way.

Objectives:
- Girls will demonstrate their knowledge of relational aggression following implementation of the relational aggression curriculum.
- Girls will demonstrate their belief systems regarding relational aggression following implementation of the relational aggression curriculum.

Procedures:
- Copy and hand out the Relational Aggression Assessment Measure located in Appendix B.
- Explain to the girls that this quiz will evaluate how their knowledge and beliefs about relational aggression have changed from the beginning group session.
- Explain that their answers will be kept confidential.

Activity 9.5: (Optional) Positive Role Models and Mentoring

Overview: Girls will become positive role models to younger girls in order to stop and prevent relational aggression.

Objectives:

- Girls will become positive role models to younger students.
- The girls will use their knowledge about relational aggression to help others.
- Girls will use the strategies learned about relational aggression to help others.
- Girls will mentor younger students to form healthy relationships with others.

Procedures:

- Develop a mentoring group for the girls who were involved in the group sessions.
- Separate the girls from this group into small groups, and assign them classrooms to teach younger students about relational aggression.
- It may be beneficial for the girls to use the projects they completed during session nine and present these projects to the younger students.
- Have the girls use Activity 9.5 Positive Role Models and Mentoring in Appendix A to help them plan what they could say to the younger students.

Presenting to Younger Students

I. **Student Presentations of Relational Aggression to Younger Students**
    A. Relational Aggression Definition and Examples
        1. Have the girls explain what relational aggression is and looks like. Have the girls use the projects they developed for the group as a guide. Girls can also use the notes and handouts from the group sessions.
        2. Allow the younger students to ask questions about relational aggression.

    B. Strategies for Relational Aggression
        1. Have the girls teach the younger students strategies for preventing and stopping relational aggression. Have the girls use the projects they developed for the group as a guide. Girls can also use the notes and handouts from the group sessions.
        2. Allow the younger students to ask questions about relational aggression.

    C. Role Play and Active Learning
        1. Have the younger students engage in real life situations, so the mentors can help the younger students problem solve through the situations. Have the girls create various relational aggression scenarios. Put these scenarios on index cards that can be handed out to the younger students to role play.
        2. Have younger students write or draw about relational aggression to show what they have learned about relational aggression from listening to the mentors.

II. **Mentoring Program**
    A. Prior to beginning the mentoring program, have the girls go through a mentor training program.
        - A sample program would include: *Meaningful Mentoring* by R. Bowman and S. Bowman
    B. Pair older girls from the relational aggression program with younger girls. Note: It may be helpful to pair girls who have a common free time (i.e. recess/lunch).
    C. Allow opportunities for the girls to meet and discuss relational aggression situations that need problem solving (i.e. before/after school or during recess/lunch time).
    D. Meet with the mentors during a designated time (i.e. recess/lunch/study hall) to check on the progress of the mentoring program and to determine the effectiveness of the program.

Leader Notes for Group Session Nine

Date: _____

Time: _____

Girls Present:

_____

_____

Girls Absent:

_____

_____

Summary of Session Nine:

_____

_____

_____

What went well:

_____

_____

_____

What did not go well and may need improvement:

_____

_____

_____

Important notes:

_____

_____

_____

_____

SESSION TEN: (OPTIONAL)

Follow Up

Purpose and Group Objectives

- Girls will demonstrate their long term knowledge of relational aggression.
- Girls will show what their beliefs and perceptions of relational aggression are.
- Girls will demonstrate strategies learned about relational aggression.
- Girls will recognize and show healthy friendship behaviors.

The purpose of this session is to determine whether there has been any long term change in the girl's knowledge and belief systems regarding relational aggression. This session should be conducted months following the last group session in order to assess for any long term changes in regards to girls' perceptions and knowledge.

Activity 10.1: Follow Up Discussion

Overview: Girls will demonstrate their retained knowledge of relational aggression. The girls will demonstrate if their beliefs about relational aggression have changed since the group meetings.

Objectives:

- Girls will demonstrate their knowledge of relational aggression following completion of the relational aggression program.
- Girls will demonstrate whether their belief systems and perceptions about relational aggression have changed following completion of this program.
- Girls will demonstrate if they have retained and utilized the strategies for dealing with relational aggression following this curriculum.

Procedures:

- Lead a discussion with the girls regarding their knowledge, perceptions, belief systems, and the strategies they have used for dealing with relational aggression. Use the discussion questions below as a guide for discussion.
- The worksheet titled Activity 10.1 in Appendix A can be reproduced and handed out to each girl. Have them write their answers to the following discussion questions on this page.

Discussion Questions:

1. What is relational aggression?
   - Relational aggression is using relationships or friendships to hurt and bully others. It is also known as female bullying.
2. What are examples of relational aggression?
   - Examples of relational aggression include: excluding others, gossiping about others, using cyber or internet bullying, spreading rumors, hurting another person's reputation, telling someone they won't be your friend unless they do what you want, etc.

3. Do you believe that relational aggression is acceptable behavior that girls just do?
   - Relational aggression is not acceptable behavior for girls or anyone. It is not okay behavior. Relational aggression will persist if girls continue to believe that it is girl behavior that all girls engage in.
4. What are some strategies for treating relational aggression?
   - Strategies include: assertiveness skills like the ACT strategy, taking responsibility for behavior, using contracts or promises, using empathy and understanding skills, taking the perspective of others, using problem solving skills like S.T.O.P., and changing thoughts about relational aggression. Being passive when relational aggression occurs is not an acceptable strategy for dealing with relational aggression. Doing nothing may send the message that relational aggression is okay behavior.

Activity 10.2: Relational Aggression Assessment Measure

Overview: Girls will demonstrate their long term knowledge about relational aggression following implementation of the relational aggression curriculum. Girls will indicate if their beliefs about relational aggression have changed in some way.

Objectives:
- Girls will demonstrate their long term knowledge of relational aggression following implementation of the relational aggression curriculum.
- Girls will demonstrate their belief systems regarding relational aggression following implementation of the relational aggression curriculum.
- Girls will demonstrate their retention of strategies for treating relational aggression following implementation of the relational aggression curriculum.

Procedures:
- Copy and hand out the Relational Aggression Assessment Measure located in Appendix B.
- Explain to the girls that this quiz will evaluate what they remember and believe about relational aggression from the last group meeting.
- Explain that their answers will be kept confidential.

Leader Notes for Group Session Ten

Date: _____

Time: _____

Girls Present:

_____

_____

Girls Absent:

_____

_____

Summary of Session Ten:

_____

_____

_____

What went well:

_____

_____

What did not go well and may need improvement:

_____

_____

_____

Important notes:

_____

_____

_____

_____

References and Resources

Bonds, M. & Stoker, S. (2000). *Bully proofing your school A comprehensive apporach for middle schools.* Longmont, CO: Sopris West.

Brown, L. M. (2004). Girlfighting: Interview with Lyn Mikel Brown. *Daughters, 9 (4),* 5-7.

Brown, L. M., Way, N., & Duff, J. (1999). The others in my I: Adolescent girls' friendships and peer relations. In N. Johnson and M. Roberts and J. Worrell (Eds.). Beyond Appearance: A New Look at Adolescent Girls (pp. 205-225). Washington, DC: American Psychological Association.

Crick, N. (1996). The role of overt aggression, relational aggression, and prosocial behavior in the prediction of children's future social adjustment. *Child Development,* 67, 2317-2327.

Crick, N., Casas, J., & Ku, H. (1999). Relational and physical forms of peer victimization in preschool. *Developmental Psychology, 35* (2), 376-385.

Crick, N., & Grotpeter, J. (1995). Relational aggression, gender, and social-psychological adjustment. *Child Development, 66,* 710-722.

Cullerton-Sen, C., Crick, N. (2005). Understanding the effects of physical and relational victimization: The utility of multiple perspectives in predicting social-emotional adjustment. *School Psychology Review,* 34, 147-160.

Debold, E., Brown, L. M., Weseen, S., & Brookins, K. G. (1999). Cultivating hardiness zones for adolescent girls: A reconceptualization of resilience in relationships with caring adults. In N. Johnson and M. Roberts and J. Worrell (Eds.). *Beyond Appearance: A New Look at Adolescent Girls* (pp. 181-204). Washington, DC: American Psychological Association.

Dellasega, C., & Nixon, C. (2003). *Girl wars: 12 strategies that will end female bullying.* New York, NY: Simon and Schuster, Incorporated.

Gewertz, C. (2003). Hand in hand. *Education Week,* 38, 39-41.

Hinshaw, S., & Lee, S. (2003). Conduct and oppositional defiant disorders. In E. Mash and R. Barkley (Eds.). *Child Psychopathology* (pp. 144-198). New York, NY: The Guilford Press.

Larson, J., & Lochman, J. E. (2002). *Helping schoolchildren cope with anger: A cognitive-behavioral intervention.* New York, New York: The Guilford Press.

Merrell, K., Carrizales, D., & Feuerborn, L. (2004). *Strong kids: A social and emotional learning curriculum for students in grades 4-8.* Eugene, OR: Oregon Resiliency Project. Retrieved from http://orp.uoregon.edu/strong%20kids.htm

Merrell, K., Juskelis, M., & Tran, O. (2004). *Evaluation of the strong kids and strong teens curricula for promoting social-emotional resilience.* Handout from a poster presentation at the annual meeting of the American Psychological Association, University of Oregon, Eugene.

McKay, C. (2003). Relational aggression in children. *Camping Magazine,* 76 (2), 5-24.

Mullin- Rindler, N. (2003). New fixes for relational aggression. *Education Digest,* 69 (1), 3-9.

Nixon, C. (2005). *RA & interventions: Reducing relationally aggressive behaviors in middle school students through intervention.* Retrieved April 8, 2005, from http://www.opheliaproject.org

Ophelia Project. (2005). *Relational aggression FAQ's.* Retrieved April 8, 2005, from http://www.opheliaproject.org/main/ra_faq.htm

Phelps, R. C. (2001). Children's responses to overt and relational aggression. *Journal of Clinical Child Psychology,* 30 (1), 240-252.

Pipher, M. (1994). *Reviving Ophelia: Saving the selves of adolescent girls.* New York, NY: The Random House Publishing Group.

Prinstein, M., Boergers, J. & Vernberg, E. (2001). Overt and relational aggression in adolescents: Social-psychological adjustment of aggressors and victims. *Journal of Clinical Child Psychology,* 30 (4), 479-491.

Rose, A., Swenson, L., & Waller, E. (2004). Overt and relational aggression and perceived popularity: Developmental differences in concurrent and prospective relations. *Developmental Psychology,* 40 (3), 378-387.

Short-Camilli, C. (1994). *Bully proofing your school: A comprehensive approach for elementary schools.* Longmont, CO: Sopris West.

Simmons, R. (2002). *Odd girl out: The hidden culture of aggression in girls.* San Diego, CA: Harcourt Trade Publishing.

Skowronski, M., Jaffe Weaver, N., & Sachs Wise, P., Kelly, R. (2005). Helping girls combat relational aggression. *Communiqué,* 33 (6), 35-37.

Wiseman, R. (2002). *Queen bees and wannabes.* New York, New York: Three Rivers Press.

Yoon, J., Barton, E., & Taiariol, J. (2004). Relational aggression in middle school: Educational implications of developmental research. *Journal of Early Adolescence,* 4 (3), 303-318.

References and Resources *Continued*

For More Information on Relational Aggression

Definition and examples of relational aggression or female bullying:

- Crick, N., & Grotpeter, J. (1995). Relational aggression, gender, and social-psychological adjustment. *Child Development, 66,* 710-722.
- Dellasega, C., & Nixon, C. (2003). *Girl wars: 12 strategies that will end female bullying.* New York, NY: Simon and Schuster, Incorporated.
- Simmons, R. (2002). *Odd girl out: The hidden culture of aggression in girls.* San Diego, CA: Harcourt Trade Publishing.
- Wiseman, R. (2002). *Queen bees and wannabes.* New York, New York: Three Rivers Press.

Definition and examples of cliques, including definition of roles in cliques:

- Simmons, R. (2002). *Odd girl out: The hidden culture of aggression in girls.* San Diego, CA: Harcourt Trade Publishing.
- Wiseman, R. (2002). *Queen bees and wannabes.* New York, NY: Three Rivers Press.

More information on assertiveness skills:

- Dellasega, C., & Nixon, C. (2003). *Girl wars: 12 strategies that will end female bullying.* New York, NY: Simon and Schuster, Incorporated.
- Simmons, R. (2002). *Odd girl out: The hidden culture of aggression in girls.* San Diego, CA: Harcourt Trade Publishing.

APPENDIX A:
Reproducible Activity Pages

Activity 1.1: Establishing Group Rules

Group Rules

1. _____
2. _____
3. _____
4. _____
5. _____

Group Signatures: I promise to keep these group rules.

_____   _____   _____

_____   _____   _____

_____   _____   _____

_____   _____   _____

_____   _____   _____

Activity 1.2: **Group Building Exercise**

Write your answer on the blanks provided below.

~~~~~~

My Favorite _____   My Favorite _____

Answer: _____   Answer: _____

After writing your answers in the blanks, fill in the circles by writing the differences
and similarities you found while listening to others.

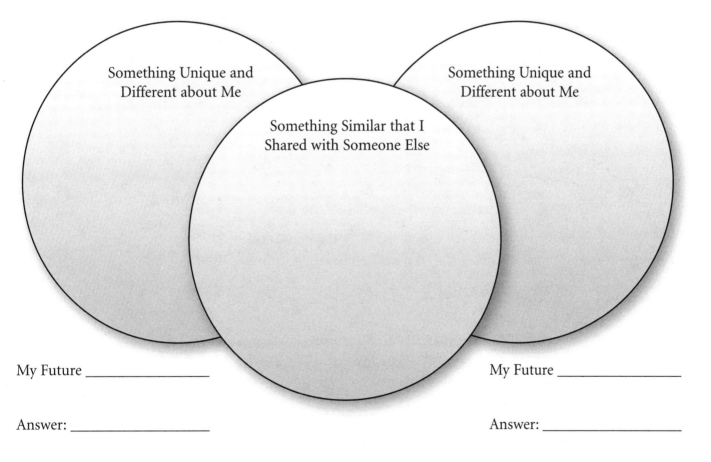

My Future _____   My Future _____

Answer: _____   Answer: _____

■ What are the benefits to being similar to or sharing something with another person?

_____

■ What are the benefits of being unique and different from someone else?

_____

A c t i v i t y 1.4: **What Do I Want to Know**

Complete the following organizer by writing your answers next to the lines provided.

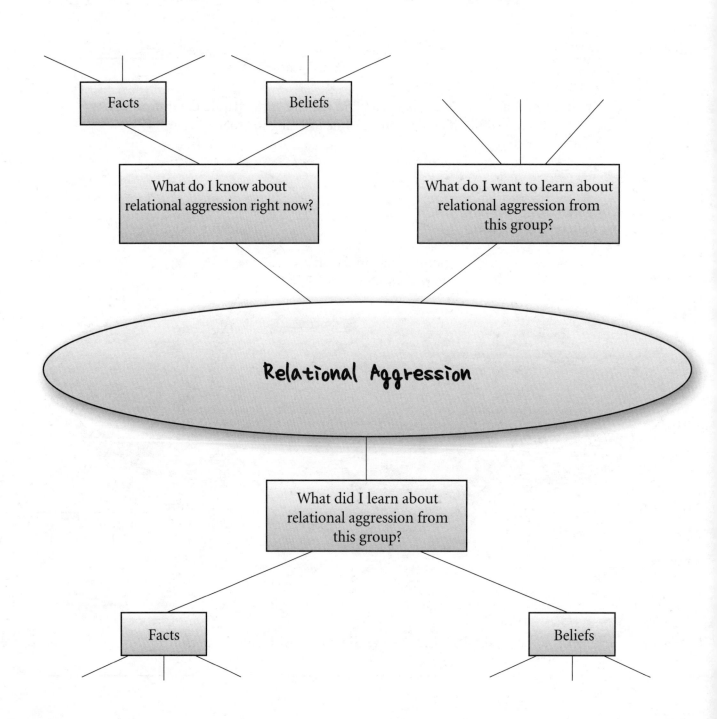

Activity 1.5: Homework — Relational Aggression

Directions: Complete the following questions by writing your answers on the blank spaces provided. Bring this sheet with you to next week's group meeting.

~~~~~~

■ What is relational aggression?

_____

_____

_____

_____

_____

_____

_____

■ What does relational aggression look like?

_____

_____

_____

_____

_____

_____

■ How does relational aggression hurt others?

_____

_____

_____

_____

_____

_____

Activity 2.1: **Mean Girl Behaviors**

Directions: Complete the following questions by writing your answers on the blanks.

1. How are girls mean to girls? What do they say? What do they do?

_____

_____

_____

_____

_____

_____

_____

_____

2. What is relational aggression? What are examples of relational aggression?

_____

_____

_____

_____

_____

_____

_____

_____

_____

Activity 2.2: **Mean Girls in Action — Movie Clip**

Directions: Complete the following questions by writing your answers on the blanks.

1. What did you see in this movie clip? Write down any thoughts you have.

_____
_____
_____
_____
_____

2. How did you see girls being mean to others? What specific things did you see?

_____
_____
_____
_____
_____

3. Who was the aggressor? Who was the victim?
How did the aggressor feel? How did the victim feel?

_____
_____
_____
_____
_____

4. What was the outcome? Did the aggressor get what she wanted by acting the way she did?

_____
_____
_____

Activity 2.3: **Relational Aggression Book Study**

Directions: Listen to a story about a girl who experienced relational aggression. After listening to this story, answer the following questions by writing your answers on the blanks.

~~~~~~

1. What was the mean behavior or relationally aggressive act observed?

_____

_____

_____

_____

_____

_____

2. Who was the victim in this passage? Who was the aggressor?

_____

_____

_____

_____

_____

_____

3. What did the victim do in this passage (i.e. were any strategies observed)?

_____

_____

_____

_____

_____

_____

4. What did the aggressor do in this passage?

_____

_____

_____

_____

_____

_____

_____

5. Who was hurt in this passage? How were they hurt?

_____

_____

_____

_____

_____

_____

_____

6. Describe any positive strategies that were used in this passage.

_____

_____

_____

_____

_____

_____

_____

_____

Activity 2.4: **Role Playing and Active Learning**

Directions: Complete this activity by writing a personal experience that you had with relational aggression on the blank. Or, create a relational aggression scenario. Choose one option.
~~~~~~

1. My relational aggression experience happened when…
   My relational aggression scenario is when…

_____

_____

_____

_____

_____

_____

_____

_____

_____

_____

■ Was it difficult to share your experience with others? Why or why not?

_____

_____

_____

_____

■ What strategies could you use in your situation or experience?

_____

_____

_____

_____

Activity 2.6: **Homework — Cliques**

Directions: Complete the following questions by writing your answers on the blanks provided. Bring this sheet with you to next week's group meeting.

~~~~~~

1. Describe what a girl group or clique is.

_____

_____

_____

_____

_____

_____

2. Do girls play certain roles in these girl groups or cliques? How?

_____

_____

_____

_____

_____

_____

_____

_____

3. What do you think is the reason girls play these roles?

_____

_____

_____

_____

_____

_____

_____

Activity 3.2: Clique Behaviors

Directions: Read each option below and check the option that applies to you. Then, complete the question at the bottom of the page.

~~~~~~

(**1.**) YES, I know what a clique or girl group is, because:

Check one or more:

_____ a.) I see cliques at school.

_____ b.) I am part of a clique at school.

_____ c.) Other _____

_____

(**2.**) NO, I don't know what a clique or girl group is, because:

Check one or more:

_____ a.) I have not seen a clique before.

_____ b.) Cliques are not in our school.

_____ c.) I have never been part of a clique.

_____ d.) Other _____

_____

■ How do cliques relate to relational aggression?

_____

_____

_____

_____

_____

_____

_____

Activity 3.3: **Influence of Friendship Groups**

Directions: Do your friendship groups influence what you do or how you think? Complete the following questions by circling yes or no. Then, answer the question at the bottom of the page.

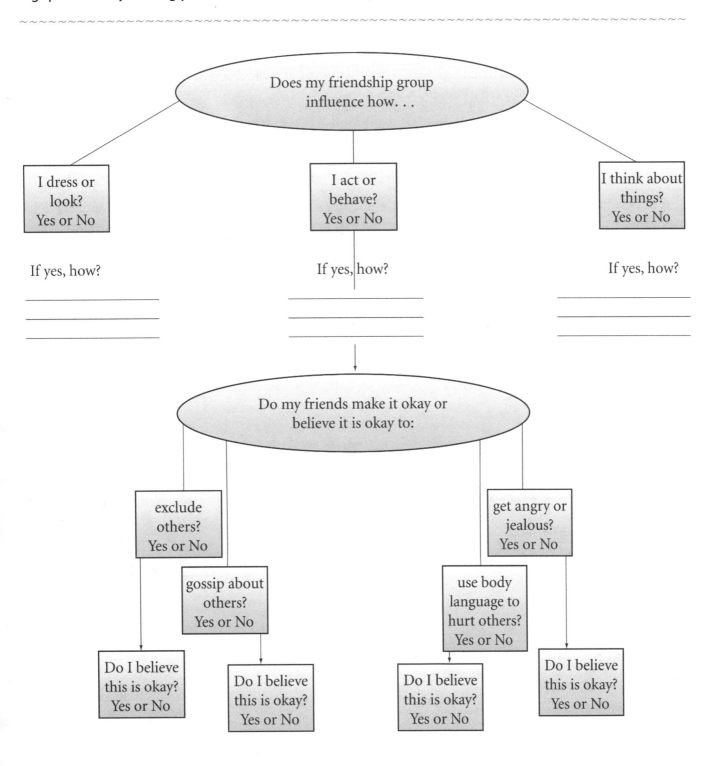

■ Are your answers the same? Do you believe what your friendship group believes?

Activity 3.4: **Role Play Scenarios**

1. One of the friends in your class got an A+ on a test when you only got a B-. You feel that you should have been the one to get an A+, because you studied harder than she did after all. She even told you that she didn't even study.

2. You just got selected to be the captain of the basketball team, which you are thrilled about. You have been practicing so hard every day. Your coach has been telling you that you are an awesome player who has a lot of talent. Your best friend, however, isn't that great at basketball and is becoming angry with you. She tells you that you are trying to be a show off.

3. This is your second week at a new school, and you notice that everyone has their certain group of friends that they hang out with during the school day. Everyone appears to be hanging out with Kelly, who is really popular and pretty. Everyone seems to like her. Making friends has never been difficult for you. You had tons of friends at your old school. You want to make new friends, but don't know how.

4. Your best friend has been kind of bossy lately, ever since she started hanging out with the popular group of girls at school and received an award for having excellent grades. She has recently told you that you could be popular too if you did what she said. She then tells you that if you don't do what she says, she's not going to invite you over to her birthday party and hang out with you anymore.

Activity 3.4: **Role Play Scenarios**

Directions: Using the role play situations provided by your group leader, read the situation and answer the following questions by writing your answers on the blanks.

~~~~~~

1. How would you handle this situation? What would you say?

_____

_____

_____

_____

_____

_____

2. How could you show self-confidence and still respect the other person's feelings?

_____

_____

_____

_____

_____

_____

3. Would it be easy to be relationally aggressive (i.e. purposely hurt someone) in this situation? How could you prevent relational aggression from happening?

_____

_____

_____

_____

_____

_____

Activity 3.5: **Girl Group Roles — Guide**

Role in Group	*Leader*
Looks Like	May want power and control, tries to make all the choices for people, complains about others, may try to initiate or start trouble, friends do what she wants, may be nice in front of adults, may blame others, does not take responsibility for actions
Why a Problem	Can have unhealthy friendships with others, may not ask for help when needs it, may have trouble trusting others, may not see how her actions are bullying and why she needs to change her behavior
Role in Group	*Girl in the Middle*
Looks Like	Uses information from all people to create conflict, tries to get others to trust her but uses information for her own good, wants to look like she isn't causing the problems but is helping everyone
Why a Problem	People may learn not to trust her, people may not want to be friends with her, may have unhealthy relationships with others, may not be confident in her own abilities and find her own values important
Role in Group	*Victim*
Looks Like	May be excluded/isolated by others, perceived to be at the bottom socially, may feel helpless and think she has no support, often rejected by others
Why a Problem	May think the bullying is her fault, may feel anxious, may want to withdraw from others, may feel lonely, may have difficulty trusting others
Role in Group	*Bystanders*
Looks Like	May not know what to do, may feel helpless and powerless, may do what others want her to do, may think she has to choose between friends
Why a Problem	May forget to value what is important to her, may be influenced to do what others think she should do, may be upset about being in this position

Activity 3.5: Girl Group Roles

Directions: Complete the following activity by writing in what the different roles are, what each role might look like, and why being in such a role can be a problem in cliques or girl groups.

~~~~~~

Role in Group _____

Looks Like _____

Why a Problem _____

Role in Group _____

Looks Like _____

Why a Problem _____

Role in Group _____

Looks Like _____

Why a Problem _____

Role in Group _____

Looks Like _____

Why a Problem _____

■ How does each role influence a girl's friendships with others? What does each girl learn about friendships or relationships?

_____

_____

_____

■ Do you play a role in a clique or girl group? If yes, which one?

_____

_____

_____

Activity 3.6: **Relational Aggression Book Study**

Directions: Listen to a story about a girl who experienced relational aggression. After listening to this story, answer the following questions by writing your answers on the blanks.

~~~~~~

1. What was the mean behavior or relationally aggressive act observed?

_____

_____

_____

_____

_____

2. Who was the victim in this passage? Who was the aggressor?

_____

_____

_____

_____

_____

_____

3. What did the victim do in this passage (i.e. were any strategies observed)?

_____

_____

_____

_____

_____

_____

4. What did the aggressor do in this passage?

_____

_____

_____

_____

_____

_____

5. Who was hurt in this passage? How were they hurt?

_____

_____

_____

_____

_____

_____

6. Describe any positive strategies that were used in this passage.

_____

_____

_____

_____

_____

_____

Activity 3.7: **Assertiveness Skills**

Directions: Read the following definition about bullying and how assertiveness strategies can help when bullying happens. Practice using the sample script below. Use this sample script when bullying happens.

~~~~~~

Relational Aggression

bullying behavior, excluding or isolating others, gossiping about others, using friendships or relationships to hurt others to get what you want, not caring about someone else's needs or wants

Passivity or Passive

doing nothing, remaining quiet or neutral about something, may appear to be accepting of the behavior

Assertiveness

not bullying behavior, getting your needs and wants met without hurting other people, stating your feelings and thoughts in an acceptable way

Assertiveness Skills

 A = **Acknowledge** the friendship and the person.

 C = **Change** the situation by telling the person what you want to be different.

 T = **Together** come up with a solution that benefits both people.

Example: "I like spending time with you and being your friend *(Acknowledge)*, but I don't like it when you talk behind my back to other people *(Change)*. I want us to get along and spend time with each other still. What can we do to make this work? Can we talk *(Together)*?"

Example: "I like that we've been friends for so long *(Acknowledge)*, but it upsets me when you tell other people not to sit with me at lunch *(Change)*. I still want to be your friend. How can we work this out so we aren't mean to each other? Can we talk about it *(Together)*?"

Role Play: "I like _____ *(Acknowledge)*, but it makes me feel _____ when _____ *(Change)*. What can we do to work this out, so we aren't mean to each other? Can we _____ *(Together)*?"

Activity 3.8: **Assertiveness Skills Practice**

Directions: Complete the chart below by writing in a current problem that you have with relational aggression, what the possible choices would be to solve the problem, and what you could say or do in real life to work the problem out.

What is the problem?	What are your choices? How can you solve this problem?	What would you say or how would you act out your choice in real life?

Activity 3.9: Behavior Contract or Promise — Example

> ### Our Group Promise
> We promise to treat everyone with respect. We will include others in our group, talk respectfully about others, and talk out our problems when we are mad at each other. We will not accept any behaviors that intentionally hurt others, including spreading rumors about others when we are mad or excluding others from our friendship group.

The Problem
Kelly and Liz were friends since kindergarten. But ever since Mary came to our school, Kelly and Liz don't get along. Kelly tries to get other people in our friendship group not to talk to Liz, and Liz tells people not to talk to Kelly. They both want Mary to be their friend and get angry when Mary wants to hang out with the other one.

People Involved in this Contract or Group Promise
Kelly, Liz, Mary

Our Choices and Action Plan
We need to talk this problem out directly with each other. We will use assertiveness strategies when we are upset or angry with someone else. Kelly and Liz need to talk about why they don't want to hang out with each other anymore. They need to read their group promise about acceptable and unacceptable behaviors when someone is mad or upset. Mary needs to also use her assertiveness skills with both girls, so she doesn't take sides.

This Contract or Promise Is Important
We want everyone to feel respected in our group. We know that when everyone is happy and getting along, we are able to have more fun as a group. Being upset with each other doesn't make anyone feel good. If everyone follows our group promise, we can talk openly with one another to solve our problems.

By signing this contract I agree to follow the group promise, and I will talk out my problems with others when I am angry.

_____   _____
Signature   *Date*

_____   _____
Signature   *Date*

_____   _____
Signature   *Date*

Activity 3.9: **Behavior Contract or Promise**

> ### Our Group Promise

The Problem

_____

_____

People Involved in this Contract or Group Promise

_____

Our Choices and Action Plan

_____

_____

This Contract or Promise Is Important

_____

_____

By signing this contract I agree to follow the group promise, and I will talk out my problems with others when I am angry.

_____   _____
Signature   Date

_____   _____
Signature   Date

_____   _____
Signature   Date

_____   _____
Signature   Date

Activity 3.10: Clique Action — Guide

Role in Group
Strategies to Use

Leader
Take responsibility for your actions by understanding that you only have control over your own actions and thoughts, recognize actions that are bullying behavior, use assertiveness vs. aggressiveness skills, use empathy skills to ask yourself how you would feel if this behavior was done to you, compliment others vs. complain about others

Role in Group
Strategies to Use

Middle Girl
Take responsibility for your actions and recognize that you are in charge of your actions, understand that joining in is bullying behavior, use self-talk to monitor your behavior (i.e. "I am acting like a bully if I take this information and gossip about someone else"), use assertiveness skills, change the subject so you aren't tempted to participate in bullying behavior, get an adult to help mediate the problem

Role in Group
Strategies to Use

Victim
Use assertiveness skills and tell the bully to stop, use humor to diffuse the situation, talk about it with someone you trust, spend time with people who are kind to you and like you for who you are, realize that the bullying is not your fault, get an adult to help

Role in Group
Strategies to Use

Bystanders
Realize that you are in control of your actions, do not join in, use assertiveness skills, help support the victim, walk away, get an adult to help mediate

Activity 3.10: Clique Action

Directions: Write down the roles that girls can play in a clique. Using the strategies you learned throughout this group, write what each girl could do to stop relational aggression from happening.

~~~~~~

Role in Group _____

Strategies to Use _____

Role in Group _____

Strategies to Use _____

Role in Group _____

Strategies to Use _____

Role in Group _____

Strategies to Use _____

- What are the strategies you talked about in your group?

_____

_____

_____

_____

_____

- Would these strategies work in real life?

_____

_____

_____

_____

_____

Activity 3.12: **Homework — Popularity**

Directions: Complete the following questions by writing your answers on the blanks provided. Bring this sheet with you to next week's group meeting.

~~~~~~

1. What does being popular mean (i.e. definitions and what does it look like)?

_____

_____

_____

2. Can you think of some advantages and disadvantages of being popular?

Advantages	Disadvantages

3. Is popularity something you want?

_____

_____

_____

4. What are you willing to do in order to be popular?

_____

_____

_____

Activity 4.1: Friendship Qualities

Directions: Complete the graphic organizer by writing what friendship means to you. Write your answers by the lines below.

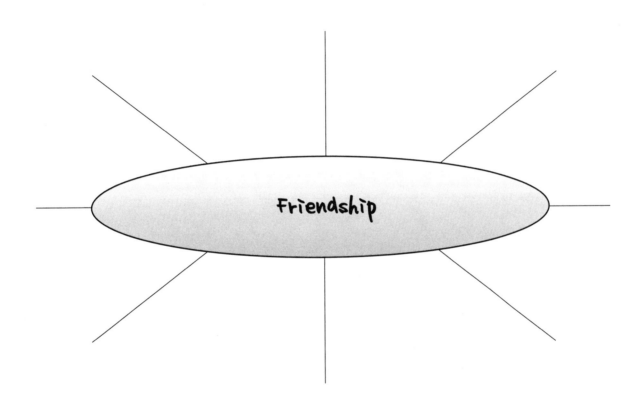

■ Summarize your graphic organizer. What does friendship mean to you? Were your ideas about friendships more positive or negative?

_____

_____

_____

_____

Activity 4.2: Friendship Qualities: Healthy vs. Unhealthy Friends

Directions: Using the graphic organizer from Activity 4.1, complete the following activity by taking your answers from Activity 4.1 and putting them in the appropriate place below.

What are some healthy qualities or positive things you listed about having friends?	What are some unhealthy qualities or negative things you listed about having friends?

Activity 4.3: Treating Others with Respect and Kindness

Directions: Read the following situations below. Decide if the action or behavior was negative or positive. Then decide if the response from others was negative or positive. If the behavior and response was negative, reframe them in a more positive way using the space provided below.

The Action or Behavior	Others Reaction or Response to the Behavior
Julie was feeling angry one day, so she decided to make one of her friends feel angry too by spreading a rumor about her. Julie thought this would make herself feel better, because someone else would be mad too.	■ When Julie's friend heard about the rumor, she was really upset. This wasn't the first time that Julie had done this to one of the girls in their friendship group. The group had tried to talk with Julie about her actions, but she still wasn't stopping the bullying behavior. So, the group finally decided that they didn't want to hang out with Julie anymore because of her constant bullying towards them. ■ Did Julie's behavior work for her? Did she get what she wanted by acting how she did? How did her friends respond to her?
Reframe:	■ How could Julie handle her feeling of anger and her actions in a more appropriate way? _____ _____ _____ _____ ■ How would others respond to her if she used a more appropriate way to show how she feels? _____ _____ _____ _____

The Action or Behavior

Others Reaction or Response to the Behavior

Erin decided to write a note about Tara. She had one of her friends give the note to Tara. Erin wrote things putting Tara down for the clothing she wore, how no one likes her, and how everybody thinks she smells.

- Tara was very upset when she received the note. She was so upset about the things written about her, that she went to the counselor to talk with her. Her teacher ended up finding about the note and talked with Erin about writing such awful things about another person. The teacher made Erin apologize and ended up calling her parents. Erin had to then talk with the counselor about her behavior. Erin's friends were also upset about the note, and they decided to tell her that they didn't like what she was doing.

- Did Erin's behavior work for her? Did she get what she wanted by acting how she did? How did her friends respond to her? What happened?

Reframe:

- How do you think Erin was feeling? What could she have done instead of writing this note about Tara to show how she felt?

  _____
  _____
  _____
  _____

- How would others respond to her if she used a more appropriate way to show how she feels?

  _____
  _____
  _____

Activity 4.4: **How People Respond to Me**

Directions: Monitor and evaluate your actions towards others. Do you act in a positive or negative way towards others? How do others respond to you when you act in a negative or positive way?

The Action or Behavior	Others Reaction or Response to the Behavior

Behavior:

■ Behavior:

_____
_____
_____

■ Did your behavior work for you? Did you get what you wanted by acting how you did? How did your friends respond to you?

_____
_____
_____

Reframe:

■ How could you change your behavior to be more positive and still get what you want?

_____
_____
_____

■ How would others respond to you if you acted more positively towards them?

_____
_____
_____

The Action or Behavior   Others Reaction or Response to the Behavior

Behavior:

■ Behavior:

_____
_____
_____
_____

■ Did your behavior work for you? Did you get what you wanted by acting how you did? How did your friends respond to you?

_____
_____
_____
_____

Reframe:

■ How could you change your behavior to be more positive and still get what you want?

_____
_____
_____
_____

■ How would others respond to you if you acted more positively towards them?

_____
_____
_____
_____

Activity 4.6: **Relational Aggression Book Study**

Directions: Listen to a story about a girl who experienced relational aggression. After listening to this story, answer the following questions by writing your answers on the blanks.

~~~~~~

1. What was the mean behavior or relationally aggressive act observed?

_____

_____

_____

_____

_____

2. Who was the victim in this passage? Who was the aggressor?

_____

_____

_____

_____

_____

3. What did the victim do in this passage (i.e. were any strategies observed)?

_____

_____

_____

_____

_____

4. What did the aggressor do in this passage?

_____

_____

_____

_____

_____

5. Who was hurt in this passage? How were they hurt?

_____

_____

_____

_____

_____

6. Describe any positive strategies that were used in this passage.

_____

_____

_____

_____

_____

Activity 4.8: **Homework — Reframing My Actions**

Directions: Complete the following questions by writing your answers on the blanks provided. Describe a time that you needed to reframe how you behaved because you acted in a negative way. Bring this sheet with you to next week's group meeting.

~~~~~~

1. What was the situation?

_____

_____

_____

_____

_____

2. What were you thinking in this situation?

_____

_____

_____

_____

_____

_____

3. How did you feel in this situation?

_____

_____

_____

_____

_____

_____

4. How did you act? What did you do?

_____

_____

_____

_____

5. How did others respond to you when you acted this way?

_____

_____

_____

_____

6. How could you have acted in a more appropriate or positive way?

_____

_____

_____

_____

7. How do you think others would have responded to you if you acted in a more positive way towards them?

_____

_____

_____

_____

Activity 5.1: Feelings and Emotions

Directions: Read the following definition about emotions. Complete the following activity by writing the correct answers in each of the boxes below.

~~~~~~

Emotion

Emotions or feelings tell us about something and allow us to change what is happening or what we are doing, emotions can be recognized mentally and physically

Mentally = our thoughts can influence how we feel about something, our feelings can also influence how we think about something (i.e. errors in thinking about a situation can happen)

Physically = our feelings might also be recognized as physical symptoms, our feelings can influence how we act physically (i.e. anxiety – the stomach might feel sick and the muscles tensed, so our anxiety mimics sickness and may influence us to leave the situation we are in)

~~~~~~

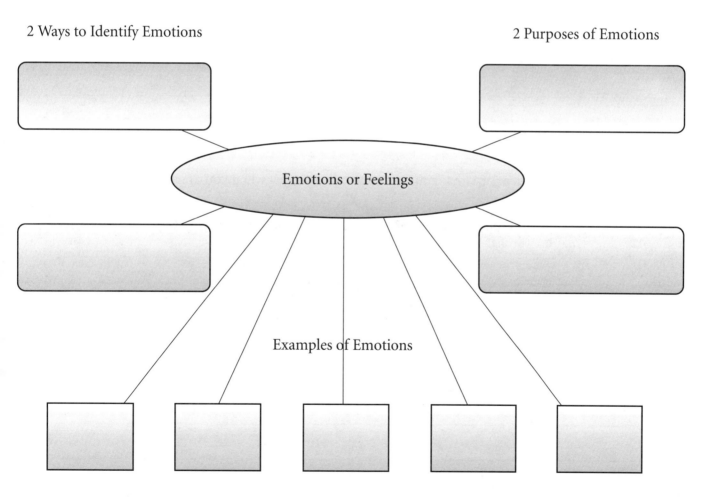

2 Ways to Identify Emotions

2 Purposes of Emotions

Emotions or Feelings

Examples of Emotions

Activity 5.2: Normal Feelings

Directions: Complete the following activity by writing your answers on the blanks provided below. List the positive and negative ways that you can show how you feel.

~~~~~~

■ Is it normal or acceptable to feel angry/mad, upset, or sad? Are these feelings okay to have?

_____

_____

_____

_____

■ Is it normal or acceptable to spread a rumor, exclude, or isolate someone when you are mad at someone? Is it okay to get revenge on someone who was mean to you?

_____

_____

_____

_____

List the positive and negative ways that you can show how you feel when you are angry with a friend.

Positive Ways to Deal with Anger	Negative Ways to Deal with Anger

Activity 5.3: **Thinking. Feeling and Relational Aggression**

Brain (Thoughts)	Feelings (Emotions)	Actions (Behavior)
"All of my friends are prettier than me."	Sad, Anxious	This girl isolates herself from being with others. She starts to spread rumors about all the girls who think they're pretty in order to feel better about herself.
"Jenny thinks that she has the best clothes in the whole class."	Jealous	This girl decides to make fun of Jenny and spreads a rumor that Jenny thinks she is better than everyone else.
"I have to be in the popular group at school or else no one will like me, and I'll be all alone."	Afraid	This girl decides to do whatever it takes to be in the popular group at school, even if it means being mean to other people in order to fit in.
"Katie didn't invite me to her party, so I'm not going to let her sit with our group at lunch."	Angry	She tells the other girls at the lunch table to exclude Katie from sitting with them.

Activity 5.3: Thinking, Feeling and Relational Aggression

Directions: Complete the following chart by filling in the thoughts, feelings, and actions about a certain situation that you have with relational aggression. Write in the blank spaces provided.

Situation

_____

_____

_____

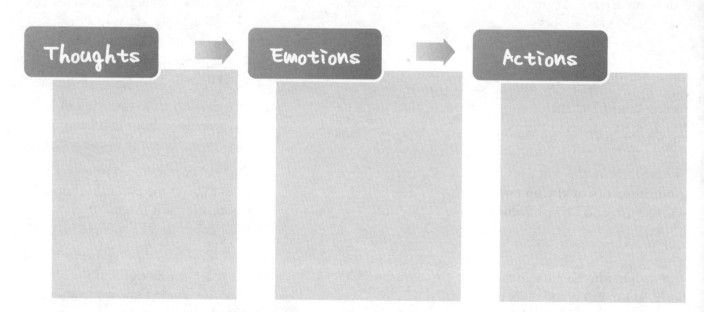

Look at your chart above. Are the thoughts, emotions, and actions you listed negative or positive? Use the chart below to turn any negative thoughts, emotions, and actions into something more positive. Write in the blank spaces provided.

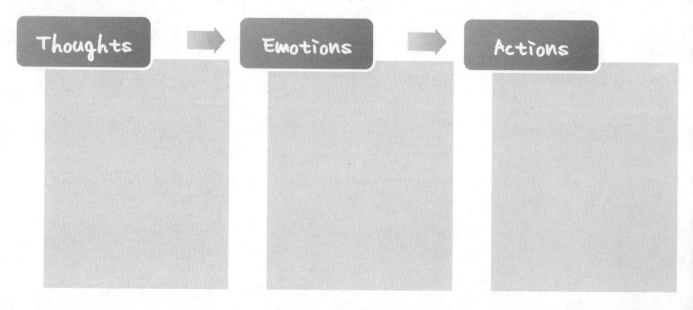

Activity 5.4: Role Play Scenarios — Understanding Feelings

Situation One
Someone in your class has been teasing you about what you are wearing and how you dress.

Situation Two
Your friend of many years begins to ignore you (i.e. gives you the silent treatment, stops talking to you) and decides to become friends with someone else.

Situation Three
You are sitting in class when a friend passes a note to another friend that you both hang out with. After your friend reads the note, they both look and laugh at you. They both begin to then whisper.

Situation Four
One of your friends asks you to hang out with them on the weekend, but you already made plans with a different friend. Your friend then becomes mad and tells you that she doesn't want to be your friend if you don't hang out with her this weekend.

Situation Five
One of your friends tells a group of your friends that she is angry with you. She then gets the group to turn against you.

Situation Six
You overhear a group of friends talking about the weekend. They say that they had an awesome time at the party you were not invited to.

Activity 5.4: **Role Play Scenarios — Understanding Feelings**

Directions: Using the role play situations provided by your group leader, read the situation and answer the following questions by writing your answers on the blanks.

~~~~~~

1. What would you think if this happened to you?

_____

_____

_____

_____

_____

2. How would you feel in this situation? What emotions would you have?

_____

_____

_____

_____

_____

3. What would you do if this happened to you?

_____

_____

_____

_____

4. List 2 positive or appropriate ways to show how you feel without hurting others.

_____

_____

_____

_____

_____

Activity 5.5: **Relational Aggression Book Study**

Directions: Listen to a story about a girl who experienced relational aggression. After listening to this story, answer the following questions by writing your answers on the blanks.

1. What was the mean behavior or relationally aggressive act observed?

_____

_____

_____

_____

_____

_____

2. Who was the victim in this passage? Who was the aggressor?

_____

_____

_____

_____

_____

_____

_____

3. What did the victim do in this passage (i.e. were any strategies observed)?

_____

_____

_____

_____

_____

_____

4. What did the aggressor do in this passage?

_____

_____

_____

_____

_____

_____

5. Who was hurt in this passage? How were they hurt?

_____

_____

_____

_____

_____

_____

_____

6. Describe any positive strategies that were used in this passage.

_____

_____

_____

_____

_____

_____

_____

Activity 5.8: **Homework — Thoughts, Feelings & Actions**

Directions: Complete the following questions by writing your answers on the blanks provided. Describe the feelings you had in a specific situation involving relational aggression. Bring this sheet with you to next week's group meeting.

~~~~~~

1. What was the situation?

_____

_____

_____

_____

2. What did you think in this situation?

_____

_____

_____

_____

3. How did you feel in this situation? What emotion did you have?

_____

_____

_____

_____

4. What did you do in the situation as a result of what you thought and felt?

_____

_____

_____

_____

Activity 6.1: **Empathy**

Directions: Read the following definition about empathy. Complete the following activity by adding empathy examples in the space provided below. Then, complete the bottom portion of this worksheet by writing your answers on the blanks provided.

~~~~~~

Empathy

understanding how another person feels or having the same emotion as another individual; having compassion for someone else; understanding another person's feelings

Examples of empathy include: asking someone to sit with you at lunch when they have no place to sit, writing a friendly note to cheer someone up, having compassion for someone who is being excluded from a group, befriending someone who is new to school

Other examples of empathy include:_____

~~~~~~

How Would You Feel? . . .   What Could You Do? . . .

A new girl at your school has no one to sit with at lunch.

(a) Has this situation ever happened to you? _____

(b) How could you show empathy in this situation? _____

_____

_____

_____

You see a group of girls whispering and staring at a girl who is in your class.

(a) Has this situation ever happened to you? _____

(b) How could you show empathy in this situation? _____

_____

_____

_____

You see a group of girls excluding another classmate from joining their group.

(a) Has this situation ever happened to you? _____

(b) How could you show empathy in this situation? _____

_____

_____

_____

Activity 6.2: **Taking the Perspective of Others**

Directions: Read what it means to take the perspective of others below. Write about someone from history and from your life that has made an impact because of the perspective they took on an issue.

Perspective of Others

looking at things from another individual's view, understanding that other people have opinions and feelings that are different even if they are in the same situation

> Different opinions are not necessarily a bad thing. Everyone is different and has something unique to contribute to the world. Different opinions can often lead to positive changes.

Think of someone from history that was discouraged from having their point of view or perspective, but ended up changing the world in an important way. List who the person was, what their point of view was, and the impact it had on the world below.

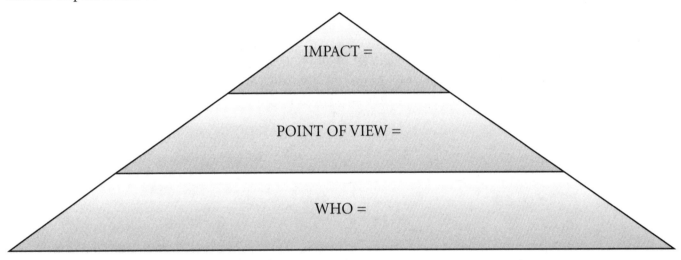

Now... think of a time in your life when you or someone in your life has had a different opinion or perspective about an issue. List who the person is, what the point of view was, and what the impact was.

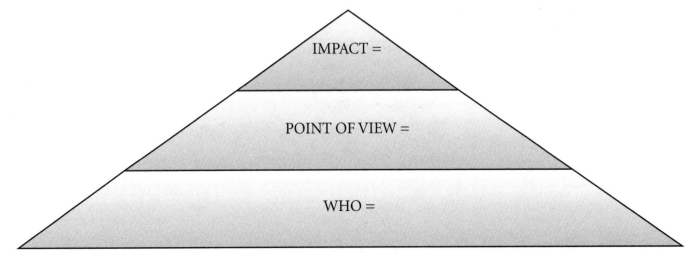

Activity 6.3: **Role Play — Empathy and the Perspective of Others Scenarios**

Situation One
You are at your locker when Tara bumps into you and says, "Oops, it was an accident" in what appears to be a sarcastic tone of voice. You begin to think to yourself that everyone hates you at this school.

Situation Two
You are walking down the hallway with your friend, Julie, who happens to be really popular. She tells you to throw a piece of gum at this girl who is always standing alone by her locker. Julie tells you that this girl thinks she's all that. Julie says she deserves it, because she never talks to anyone and keeps to herself.

Situation Three
You are one of the most popular girls in school. You are standing in the lunch line with your friends laughing at a funny joke. Erika walks by at that moment and gives you a dirty look. You automatically think that Erika must be mad at you.

Situation Four
It is the first day of your new school. You walk into the lunchroom and try to find a place to sit down. You look over and see Shawna, a girl from your homeroom class, looking at you. She turns to a group of girls and starts laughing. You automatically think Shawna is laughing at you.

Activity 6.3: **Role Play — Empathy and the Perspective of Others Scenarios**

Directions: Using the role play situations provided by your group leader, read the situation and answer the following questions by writing your answers on the blanks.

~~~~~~

1. How would each person probably feel in your scenario? List the emotions below.

You Would Probably Feel	Tara/Julie/Erika/Shawna Would Probably Feel

2. Are there any clues that tell you how each person might feel? What are they?

_____

_____

_____

3. Would everyone feel the same way if this happened to them? Why or why not?

_____

_____

_____

4. Why is it important to see things from the perspective of others?

_____

_____

_____

5. How could you show empathy in each of these scenarios?

_____

_____

_____

Activity 6.4: **Relational Aggression Book Study**

Directions: Listen to a story about a girl who experienced relational aggression. After listening to this story, answer the following questions by writing your answers on the blanks.

~~~~~~

1. What was the mean behavior or relationally aggressive act observed?

_____

_____

_____

_____

_____

2. Who was the victim in this passage? Who was the aggressor?

_____

_____

_____

_____

_____

_____

3. What did the victim do in this passage (i.e. were any strategies observed)?

_____

_____

_____

_____

_____

_____

4. What did the aggressor do in this passage?

_____

_____

_____

_____

_____

_____

_____

5. Who was hurt in this passage? How were they hurt?

_____

_____

_____

_____

_____

_____

_____

6. Describe any positive strategies that were used in this passage.

_____

_____

_____

_____

_____

_____

_____

Activity 6.6: **Homework — Perspective Change**

Directions: Complete the following questions by writing your answers on the blanks provided. Describe a specific time when your perspective changed about something. Bring this sheet with you to next week's group meeting.

~~~~~~

1. What was the situation?

_____

_____

_____

_____

2. How did your perspective change?

_____

_____

_____

_____

_____

3. What did you think in this situation?

_____

_____

_____

_____

4. How did you feel in this situation?

_____

_____

_____

_____

_____

Activity 7.1: **Unique Me**

Directions: Complete this activity by listing the abilities, characteristics, strengths, and roles you play that make you unique by the lines below.

~~~~~~

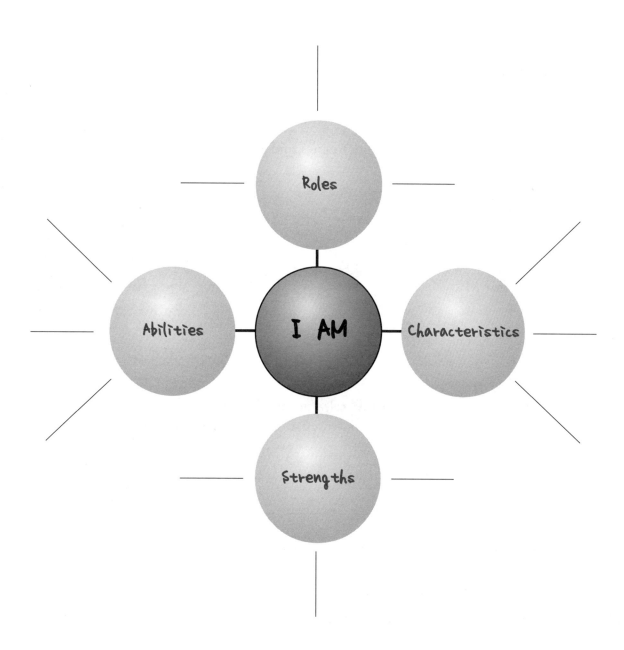

Activity 7.2: My Self-Esteem and Self-Talk

Directions: Complete this activity by writing your answers to each of the questions below.

~~~~~~

■ What is self-esteem? What does being self-confident mean?

_____

_____

_____

_____

Fill in the following chart by writing the thoughts, feelings, and goals you have for yourself in the spaces below.

What I Think About Myself:	How I Feel About Myself:
My Self-Talk	
The Goals I Have For Myself:	Do Others Influence How I Feel About Me:

■ Rate your self-esteem. Do you have a positive self-esteem about yourself (i.e. What are your thoughts and feelings about yourself? Do you accept constructive criticism? Do you recognize what your strengths and weaknesses are?)

_____

_____

_____

_____

■ How does self-esteem and self-confidence relate to relational aggression? Do people with self-confidence and a positive self-esteem feel the need to bully others?

_____

_____

_____

_____

Activity 7.3: My Self-View: Who I Want to Be

Directions: Write your answers to the questions below. Write your responses in the space provided. Then, answer the questions at the bottom of this worksheet.

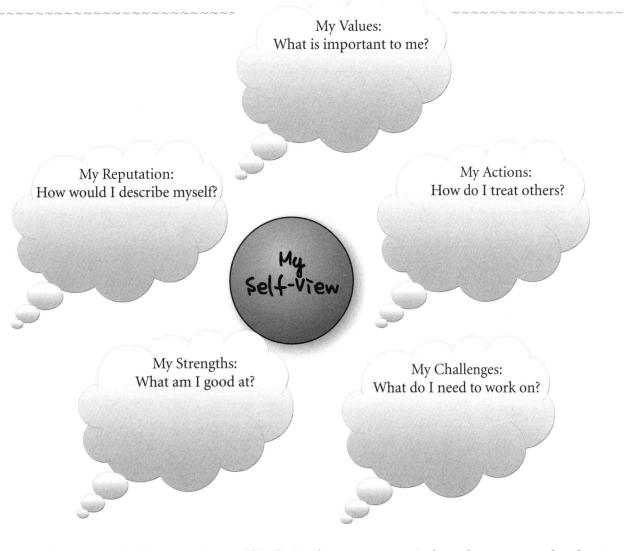

My Values:
What is important to me?

My Reputation:
How would I describe myself?

My Actions:
How do I treat others?

My Self-View

My Strengths:
What am I good at?

My Challenges:
What do I need to work on?

■ Are your actions toward others positive and kind? Or, do you act negatively and mean towards others?

_____

_____

■ What is your reputation with others?

_____

_____

■ Do your actions towards others, and towards yourself, match how you want others to view you?

_____

_____

Activity 7.5: **Relational Aggression Book Study**

Directions: Listen to a story about a girl who experienced relational aggression. After listening to this story, answer the following questions by writing your answers on the blanks.

1. What was the mean behavior or relationally aggressive act observed?

_____

_____

_____

_____

_____

_____

2. Who was the victim in this passage? Who was the aggressor?

_____

_____

_____

_____

_____

_____

_____

3. What did the victim do in this passage (i.e. were any strategies observed)?

_____

_____

_____

_____

_____

_____

4. What did the aggressor do in this passage?

_____

_____

_____

_____

_____

_____

5. Who was hurt in this passage? How were they hurt?

_____

_____

_____

_____

_____

_____

6. Describe any positive strategies that were used in this passage.

_____

_____

_____

_____

_____

_____

Activity 7.7: Homework — Influences of kindness

Directions: Complete the following questions by writing your answers on the blanks provided. Describe what the act of kindness was and evaluate how it went. Bring this sheet with you to next week's group meeting.

~~~~~~

1. What was the act of kindness on your index card?

_____

_____

_____

2. What was the situation? When did you act out what was written on your card?

_____

_____

_____

_____

3. What did you think about the situation?

_____

_____

_____

4. How did you feel about the situation?

_____

_____

_____

5. How did the other person respond to you after you were nice to them?

_____

_____

_____

_____

Activity 8.1: **Problem Solving and My Belief System (Worksheet #1)**

Directions: Use the example situation on the following page to answer the four questions below. Use the problem solving steps, STOP.

~~~~~~

1. (S) What was the *Situation* or problem that this girl faced?

_____

_____

_____

2. (T) What was the girl's *Thought* or belief in this situation?

_____

_____

_____

3. (O) What *Options* did she think of in this situation? What did she decide to do?

_____

_____

_____

_____

4. (P) What was the *Progress* or outcome because of the choice she made? Did it work or does she need to try another option?

_____

_____

_____

_____

~~~~~~

S = *Situation*: What is the situation or problem?

T = *Thoughts*: What am I thinking in this situation?

O = *Options*: What can I choose to do? What would happen next?

P = *Progress*: Did my choice work? Do I need to do something else?

~~~~~~

Activity 8.1: **Problem Solving and My Belief System Chart (Worksheet #2)**

Situation or Problem	**T**hought or Belief	**F**eeling or Emotion	**O**ptions and Decision Making		**P**rogress and Outcome
			Options:	*What Would Happen Next?*	*How Did My Option Work?*
You were not invited to a party over the past weekend. You overheard two girls talking about how fun the party was.	You think that you weren't invited to the party, because no one really likes you.	You are **angry** about the situation. You are also upset about the situation.	You could exclude her from coming to your next party.	This could make her mad and upset too, but I would be acting like a bully if I did this.	If I would have excluded her from coming to one of my parties or spread a rumor about her, I would have been acting like a bully. This could have made things worse, too. Maybe people would end up not liking me, because I was being mean towards others.
			You could spread a rumor that no one likes her and wants to be her friend.	Maybe people wouldn't like her, but I would be acting like a bully if I did this. Plus, people might not like me for spreading rumors.	
			*You could talk with her up front and use assertiveness skills (i.e. ACT strategy) to tell how I feel.	I don't want to be a bully, and this would be the best choice to handle this situation.	When I used my assertiveness skills, we were able to talk things out. I found out it was an accident that I didn't get invited. We decided to sign a friendship contract or promise and always discuss things in this way in the future.

Activity 8.2: **Problem Solving in Action**

Directions: Use the blank chart to solve one of your own situations with relational aggression. Go through each of the problem solving steps and write your answers in the chart.

~~~~~~

1. **(S)** What was the *Situation* or problem that you faced?

2. **(T)** What was your *Thought* or belief in this situation?

3. **(O)** What *Options* did you think of in this situation? What did you decide to do?

4. **(P)** What was the *Progress* or outcome because of the choice you made? Did it/would it work or do you need to try another option?

Activity 8.2: **Problem Solving and My Belief System Chart**

Situation or Problem	**T**hought or Belief	**F**eeling or Emotion	**O**ptions and Decision Making		**P**rogress and Outcome
			Options:	*What Would Happen Next?*	*How Did My Option Work?*

Activity 8.3: **Relational Aggression Book Study**

Directions: Listen to a story about a girl who experienced relational aggression. After listening to this story, answer the following questions by writing your answers on the blanks.

~~~~~~

1. What was the mean behavior or relationally aggressive act observed?

_____

_____

_____

_____

_____

2. Who was the victim in this passage? Who was the aggressor?

_____

_____

_____

_____

_____

_____

3. What did the victim do in this passage (i.e. were any strategies observed)?

_____

_____

_____

_____

_____

_____

4. What did the aggressor do in this passage?

_____

_____

_____

_____

_____

_____

5. Who was hurt in this passage? How were they hurt?

_____

_____

_____

_____

_____

_____

_____

6. Describe any positive strategies that were used in this passage.

_____

_____

_____

_____

_____

_____

_____

Activity 9.2: **Setting Goals**

~~~~~~

M Y   G O A L   S H E E T

Goal =

A goal is something that I want and is realistic for me to get. It is something that I will work for.
Goals can be short term (right now) or long term (future). Goals can be academic and/or behavioral.

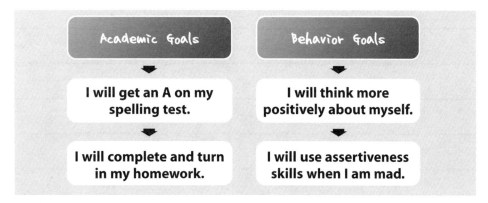

What are some goals that you want to achieve? List them in the spaces below.

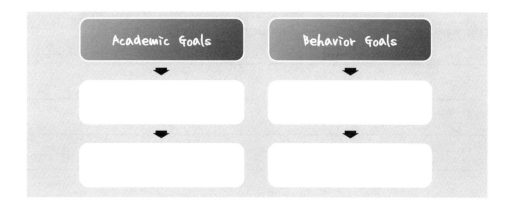

Goal Setting =

Goal setting is a process or a way to get your goals. Fill in the goal setting steps below to reach one of
the goals you listed above.

G = _____

     GET what I want   (What do I want to work for or achieve?)

O = _____, _____, _____, _____

     OPTIONS to get goal   (What do I have to do to get it? Is it possible for me?)

A = _____

     ACTION or act   (Which option did I choose? Do it!)

L = _____

     LOOK and learn   (Did I get my goal? Or, what do I have to do next?)

Activity 9.5: (Optional) Positive Role Models and Mentoring

Directions: Teach younger students about relational aggression. Mentor younger students by helping them work through relationally aggressive situations by using the strategies you learned in this group.

Use the following questions to help you prepare what you could say as a mentor to younger students.

~~~~~~

1. What is relational aggression? What does it look like?

_____

_____

_____

_____

_____

_____

2. What would you want someone else to know about relational aggression?

_____

_____

_____

_____

_____

_____

3. How could you teach someone else about relational aggression? What activities would you want to include?

_____

_____

_____

_____

_____

_____

4. What strategies would you teach someone for stopping and preventing relational aggression?

_____

_____

_____

_____

_____

_____

Notes:

_____

_____

_____

_____

_____

_____

_____

_____

_____

_____

_____

_____

_____

_____

_____

Activity 10.1 (Optional): **Follow Up Discussion**

Directions: Complete the following questions by writing your answers on the space provided.

~~~~~~

1. What is relational aggression?

_____
_____
_____
_____
_____

2. What are examples of relational aggression?

_____
_____
_____
_____
_____
_____

3. Do you believe that relational aggression is acceptable behavior that girls just do?

_____
_____
_____
_____
_____
_____

4. What are some strategies for treating relational aggression?

_____

_____

_____

_____

_____

_____

_____

5. Have you used any of these strategies? If so, which ones and have they worked?

_____

_____

_____

_____

_____

_____

_____

6. What is something specific that has helped you from being in this group?

_____

_____

_____

_____

_____

_____

APPENDIX B:

Relational Aggression
Student Assessment Measure

Name: _____

Grade: _____

Age: _____

Date: _____

~~~~~~

Directions:

Read the following questions to yourself and answer them by circling your answer. Choose the **ONE** answer that you think is the best answer. If you are unsure about a question, choose the answer that you feel makes the most sense. **There are two parts.** Please make sure you answer all of the questions.

_____   _____

Pretest Score   Posttest Score

Part One: Relational Aggression Knowledge

1. Relational aggression is using relationships or friendships to hurt others.
   a. True   b. False

2. Examples of relational aggression include:
   a. excluding someone on purpose
   b. telling someone you won't be their friend if they don't do what you want
   c. spreading a rumor about someone else
   d. all of the above are examples
   e. I don't know what relational aggression is

3. Relational aggression can also be called female bullying.
   a. True   b. False

4. Rolling your eyes, or using body language, when others are talking can be an example of relational aggression.
   a. True   b. False

5. Children as young as preschool can show relational aggression.
   a. True   b. False

6. Ignoring someone on purpose can be an example of relational aggression.
   a. True   b. False

7. Being jealous of others can lead to relational aggression.
   a. True   b. False

8. Fearing rejection, or not being part of a group, can be a reason that girls are mean to others.
   a. True   b. False

9. Being part of a popular group in school protects a girl from being left out or being talked about behind her back.
   a. True   b. False

10. Doing nothing, or being passive, when girls are mean to others is the best way to handle relational aggression when it happens.
    a. True   b. False

11. Girls who are mean to others may often act nice in front of adults.
    a. True   b. False

12. If I don't agree with my friend and want to tell them in a positive way, I could use assertiveness skills like the ACT strategy.
    a. True   b. False

13. The ACT strategy is:
    a. admitting you were wrong, changing what you are doing, and telling the person you are sorry
    b. acting nice to the person who made you mad, complaining to another friend about the problem, and telling the person you do not want to be friends
    c. acting like nothing is wrong, correcting your behavior, and telling yourself everything is fine
    d. acknowledging the person or friendship by saying something good, asking the person to change what they are doing, and together come up with a solution to end things in a positive or good way

14. Relational aggression may lead to isolation (or wanting to always being alone), depression (feeling sad for a long time), and/or anxiety (constantly worrying about things).
    a. True b. False

15. Boys and girls can be mean to each other in different ways.
    a. True b. False

16. Cliques are exclusive or selective groups of girls that hang out together.
    a. True b. False

17. Cliques can have specific rules that must be followed in order to be a part of their group.
    a. True b. False

18. There can be specific roles (i.e. Group Leader, Girl in the Middle, Victim, Bystander) in girl groups or cliques.
    a. True b. False

19. A good way to stop relational aggression is to:
    a. tell the person what the problem is in a good way
    b. ask the person to change their behavior
    c. work together to come up with a positive solution or answer to the problem
    d. all of the above
    e. none of the above

20. A contract or promise can be a strategy to use when relational aggression happens.
    a. True b. False

21. An emotion:
    a. is a feeling
    b. tells you something
    c. can help you recognize when you need to make a change
    d. all of the above
    e. none of the above

22. Empathy is understanding someone else's feelings or feeling the same emotion as they do.
    a. True b. False

23. An example of showing empathy towards someone is:
    a. telling someone it is okay when they are feeling down
    b. writing someone a friendly note when they are upset
    c. asking someone to sit with you during lunch when they are alone
    d. all of the above are examples
    e. none of the above are examples

24. Being aggressive means expressing your needs, or getting what you want, in a way that hurts others.
    a. True b. False

25. Being assertive means expressing your feelings, thoughts, rights, and needs in a way that doesn't hurt other people.
    a. True b. False

26. Which of the following are strategies for dealing with relational aggression:
   a. ACT strategy
   b. assertiveness skills
   c. showing empathy towards someone else
   d. problem solving strategies
   e. all of the above

27. What does STOP stand for?
   a. signal, together, output, plan
   b. situation, thought, options, progress
   c. surprise, turn-taking, outcome, purpose
   d. none of the above

28. What is a goal?
   a. something you are willing to work for
   b. something that you want
   c. something that can be short term (or right now)
   d. something that can be long term (or for the future)
   e. all of the above
   f. none of the above

Part Two: Relational Aggression Beliefs

1. I believe that excluding others (i.e. not letting others in my friendship group) is okay.
    a. Yes   **b.** No

2. I believe that it is okay to talk behind someone's back when I am mad.
    a. Yes   **b.** No

3. It is better to talk with your friend when you are mad at them instead of telling someone else about it.
    a. Yes   **b.** No

4. I exclude others at times.
    a. Yes   **b.** No

5. It is okay to hurt someone's feelings if I can get into the popular group at school.
    a. Yes   **b.** No

6. I believe that it is okay to ignore someone on purpose.
    a. Yes   **b.** No

7. I often spread rumors about people to fit in with my friendship group.
    a. Yes   **b.** No

8. I am friends with people who want me to be exclusive (i.e. be only with them) in their group.
    a. Yes   **b.** No

9. I feel that I always have to control (i.e. tell them what to do) my friends.
    a. Yes   **b.** No

10. I feel that I have to be friends with everyone.
    a. Yes   **b.** No

11. I feel that I have to respect the rights of everyone.
    a. Yes   **b.** No

12. I feel that I have control over my thoughts and beliefs.
    a. Yes   **b.** No

13. I feel that I have control over my behavior or actions.
    a. Yes   **b.** No

14. It is important to understand the perspective of others.
    a. Yes   **b.** No

15. I appreciate that everyone is unique and different.
    a. Yes   **b.** No

16. I use assertiveness skills to solve my friendship problems.
    a. Yes   **b.** No

APPENDIX C:

Relational Aggression Assessment Measure (Leader Guide)

Name: _____

Grade: _____

Age: _____

Date: _____

~~~~~~

Directions:

Read the following questions to yourself and answer them by circling your answer. Choose the **ONE** answer that you think is the best answer. If you are unsure about a question, choose the answer that you feel makes the most sense. **There are two parts.** Please make sure you answer all of the questions.

_____   _____

Pretest Score   Posttest Score

Part One: Relational Aggression Knowledge

1. Relational aggression is using relationships or friendships to hurt others.
   a. True b. False

2. Examples of relational aggression include:
   a. excluding someone on purpose
   b. telling someone you won't be their friend if they don't do what you want
   c. spreading a rumor about someone else
   d. all of the above are examples
   e. I don't know what relational aggression is

3. Relational aggression can also be called female bullying.
   a. True b. False

4. Rolling your eyes, or using body language, when others are talking can be an example of relational aggression.
   a. True b. False

5. Children as young as preschool can show relational aggression.
   a. True b. False

6. Ignoring someone on purpose can be an example of relational aggression.
   a. True b. False

7. Being jealous of others can lead to relational aggression.
   a. True b. False

8. Fearing rejection, or not being part of a group, can be a reason that girls are mean to others.
   a. True b. False

9. Being part of a popular group in school protects a girl from being left out or being talked about behind her back.
   a. True **b. False**

10. Doing nothing, or being passive, when girls are mean to others is the best way to handle relational aggression when it happens.
    a. True **b. False**

11. Girls who are mean to others may often act nice in front of adults.
    a. True b. False

12. If I don't agree with my friend and want to tell them in a positive way, I could use assertiveness skills like the ACT strategy.
    a. True b. False

13. The ACT strategy is:
    a. admitting you were wrong, changing what you are doing, and telling the person you are sorry
    b. acting nice to the person who made you mad, complaining to another friend about the problem, and telling the person you do not want to be friends
    c. acting like nothing is wrong, correcting your behavior, and telling yourself everything is fine
    d. acknowledging the person or friendship by saying something good, asking the person to change what they are doing, and together come up with a solution to end things in a positive or good way

14. Relational aggression may lead to isolation (or wanting to always be alone), depression (feeling sad for a long time), and/or anxiety (worrying about things).
  a. True b. False

15. Boys and girls can be mean to each other in different ways.
  a. True b. False

16. Cliques are exclusive or selective groups of girls that hang out together.
  a. True b. False

17. Cliques can have specific rules that must be followed in order to be a part of their group.
  a. True b. False

18. There can be specific roles (i.e. Group Leader, Girl in the Middle, Victim, Bystander) in girl groups or cliques.
  a. True b. False

19. A good way to stop relational aggression is to:
  a. tell the person what the problem is in a good way
  b. ask the person to change their behavior
  c. work together to come up with a positive solution or answer to the problem
  d. all of the above
  e. none of the above

20. A contract or promise can be a strategy to use when relational aggression happens.
  a. True b. False

21. An emotion:
  a. is a feeling
  b. tells you something
  c. can help you recognize when you need to make a change
  d. all of the above
  e. none of the above

22. Empathy is understanding someone else's feelings or feeling the same emotion as they do.
  a. True b. False

23. An example of showing empathy towards someone is:
  a. telling someone it is okay when they are feeling down
  b. writing someone a friendly note when they are upset
  c. asking someone to sit with you during lunch when they are alone
  d. all of the above are examples
  e. none of the above are examples

24. Being aggressive means expressing your needs, or getting what you want, in a way that hurts others.
  a. True b. False

25. Being assertive means expressing your feelings, thoughts, rights, and needs in a way that doesn't hurt other people.
  a. True b. False

26. Which of the following are strategies for dealing with relational aggression:
    a. ACT strategy
    b. assertiveness skills
    c. showing empathy towards someone else
    d. problem solving strategies
    e. **all of the above**

27. What does STOP stand for?
    a. signal, together, output, plan
    b. **situation, thought, options, progress**
    c. surprise, turn-taking, outcome, purpose
    d. none of the above

28. What is a goal?
    a. something you are willing to work for
    b. something that you want
    c. something that can be short term (or right now)
    d. something that can be long term (or for the future)
    e. **all of the above**
    f. none of the above

~~~~~~

Assessment Measure Interpretation

Total points possible = 28

Pretest - record the total number of points received on the front page of the Relational Aggression Assessment Measure on the pretest blank

Posttest – record the total number of points received on the front page of the Relational Aggression Assessment Measure on the posttest blank

~~~~~~

Interpretation - an increase in the total number of points received from the pretest to the posttest suggests an increase in knowledge of relational aggression and the strategies to use for treating relational aggression

Part Two: Relational Aggression Beliefs

1. I believe that excluding others (i.e. not letting others in my friendship group) is okay.
   a. Yes = 0   **b.** No = 1

2. I believe that it is okay to talk behind someone's back when I am mad.
   a. Yes = 0   **b.** No = 1

3. It is better to talk with your friend when you are mad at them instead of telling someone else about it.
   a. Yes = 1   **b.** No = 1

4. I exclude others at times.
   a. Yes = 0   **b.** No = 1

5. It is okay to hurt someone's feelings if I can get into the popular group at school.
   a. Yes = 0   **b.** No = 1

6. I believe that it is okay to ignore someone on purpose.
   a. Yes = 0   **b.** No = 1

7. I often spread rumors about people to fit in with my friendship group.
   a. Yes = 0   **b.** No = 1

8. I am friends with people who want me to be exclusive (i.e. be only with them) in their group.
   a. Yes = 0   **b.** No = 1

9. I feel that I always have to be in control or tell my friends what to do.
   a. Yes = 0   **b.** No = 1

10. I feel that I have to be friends with everyone.
    a. Yes = 0   **b.** No = 1

11. I feel that I have to respect the rights of everyone.
    a. Yes = 1   **b.** No = 0

12. I feel that I have control over my thoughts and beliefs.
    a. Yes = 1   **b.** No = 0

13. I feel that I have control over my behavior or actions.
    a. Yes = 1   **b.** No = 0

14. It is important to understand the perspective of others.
    a. Yes = 1   **b.** No = 0

15. I appreciate that everyone is unique and different.
    a. Yes = 1   **b.** No = 0

16. I use assertiveness skills to solve my friendship problems.
    a. Yes = 1   **b.** No = 0

~~~~~~

Assessment Measure Interpretation

Total points possible = 16

Pretest - record the total number of points received on the front page of the Relational Aggression Assessment Measure on the pretest blank

Posttest – record the total number of points received on the front page of the Relational Aggression Assessment Measure on the posttest blank

~~~~~~

Interpretation:

14-16 points = possibly suggests that girls believe that it is not okay to exclude others, talk behind other peoples' backs, ignore people on purpose, hurt someone's feelings in order to be popular, or spread rumors about others; believes that it is important to take the perspective of others; believes that one has control over their own thinking and behaviors

12-13 points = might indicate that girls believe some relationally aggressive behaviors are acceptable given a certain situation, one might think that it is okay to exclude or ignore people on purpose when it is done to them; one might believe that outside circumstances control one's thoughts and behaviors

0-11 points = might suggest that one does not understand how relationally aggressive behaviors can be hurtful to others as well as to the individual herself; might suggest inappropriate strategies and coping mechanisms for dealing with relational aggression; may need to develop a more appropriate belief system regarding relational aggression

APPENDIX D:

Relational Aggression Small Group Screening Form

Please identify the names of girls currently in attendance in the general education program, and who are NOT currently in psychological treatment in or outside of the school, and who meet two (2) or more of the following characteristics:

1. She is often the target of or initiates mean-spirited teasing

2. She is often left out of social events or excludes others from social events

3. She is often seen alone or needs to be a leader over a group of girls

4. She often complains about verbal misbehavior (i.e. gossip, rumors)

Place an * by the name if you are unsure if she is currently in psychological treatment

Name(s)	Grade	Homeroom

APPENDIX E:
Relational Aggression Book Study Suggestions

Option One

Hand out the same book to each girl for a book study. During each group session, read a selected passage from this book. Have the girls complete the worksheet activities that correspond to each group session.

Option Two

Use the selected books and passages listed below. Or, select your own passage from the suggested books. Have the girls complete the worksheet activities that correspond to each group session.

- Session Two: Relational Aggression: Definitions and Examples
  - Middle to High School: *Odd Girl Speaks Out* (pages 18-24) by R. Simmons
  - Lower to Upper Elementary: *My Secret Bully* by T. Ludwig
- Session Three: Relational Aggression: Cliques, Girl Groups, & Popularity
  - Middle to High School: *Odd Girl Speaks Out* (pages 68-70; 88-93) by R. Simmons
  - Lower to Upper Elementary: *The English Roses* by Madonna
- Session Four: Against Relational Aggression: Developing Healthy Friendships
  - Middle to High School: *Girl Wars: 12 Strategies That Will End Female Bullying* (pages 58-59) by C. Dellasega and C. Nixon
  - Lower to Upper Elementary: *The Recess Queen* by A. O'Neill
- Session Five: Healthy Socio-Emotional Behaviors: Relational Aggression and Feelings
  - Middle to High School: *Girl Wars: 12 Strategies That Will End Female Bullying* (pages 84-86) by C. Dellasega and C. Nixon
  - Lower to Upper Elementary: *On Monday When It Rained* by C. Kachenmeister
- Session Six: Healthy Socio-Emotional Behaviors: Relational Aggression and Empathy
  - Middle to High School: *Girl Wars: 12 Strategies That Will End Female Bullying* (pages 52-53, 161-162) by C. Dellasega and C. Nixon
  - Lower to Upper Elementary: *Say Something* by P. Moss
- Session Seven: Against Relational Aggression: Building Self-Confidence
  - Middle to High School: *Girl Wars: 12 Strategies That Will End Female Bullying* (pages 124-126) by C. Dellasega and C. Nixon
  - Lower to Upper Elementary: *Dancing in the Wings* by K. Nelson
- Session Eight: Against Relational Aggression: Challenging Negative Beliefs
  - Middle to High School: *Girl Wars: 12 Strategies That Will End Female Bullying* (pages 167-170) by C. Dellasega and C. Nixon
  - Lower to Upper Elementary: *Alley Oops* by J. Levy

Reading Literature about Relational Aggression

How Not To Be A Bully Target	Grades 3-6
The Recess Queen	Grades 1-5
My Secret Bully	Grades K-6
Blue Cheese Breath and Stinky Feet	Grades K-6
Bootsie Barker Ballerina	Grades K-5
Emily Breaks Free	Grades K-5
Just a Bully	Grades K-5
Stop Picking On Me	Grades K-4
Seemor's Flight To Freedom	Grades K-4
Nobody Knew What To Do	Grades K-4
Don't Laugh At Me	Grades PK-3

Resources for Educators and Parents

Girl Wars: 12 Strategies that Will End Female Bullying	Grades 6-12
Queen Bees and Wannabes	Grades 6-12
Odd Girl Out; Odd Girl Speaks Out	Grades 6-12
Mean Chicks, Cliques, and Dirty Tricks	Grades 6-12
No Room for Bullies	Grades 5-12
The Bully, The Bullied, and Beyond	Grades 5-12
Bullying in the Girls World	Grades 3-8
How to Handle Bullies, Teasers, and Other Meanies	Grades K-8
The Bully Free Classroom	Grades K-8

About the Author

Jamie M. Kupkovits, Ed.S., NCSP, is a nationally
certified school psychologist. She currently works as
a school psychologist in Wisconsin. She has an
Education Specialist Degree and a Masters Degree in
Education from the school psychology program at the
University of Wisconsin-Whitewater. Jamie has
presented research on relational aggression and her
school-based intervention program. Her primary
research interests include relational aggression
awareness and intervention, prevention and early
intervention, and the evaluation of school-based
intervention. She resides in Waukesha, Wisconsin
with her husband, Thor.